Ten years ago, I had the privilege ⟨...⟩ trey's sermon series on the often-overlooked book of Nehemiah. Because of this study, those pages of my Bible are covered in handwritten notes, quotes, lessons, and highlights that I ponder and pray over to this day. What a thrill to discover that this sermon series has been reborn for small groups and bible studies. As I read through the devotionals and personal testimonies, I was struck again by Michael's extraordinary ability to present the full weight of the Old Testament in the context of history, yet make Nehemiah's dramatic journey applicable and inspirational today. Once again, I was immersed in the transformational concept of holy discontent, and how to use it to cultivate faith and build hope in my own life, and in others. For me, both in person and on paper, this well-written and beautifully organized study was truly life-changing."

—Roxanne St. Claire, *New York Times* and *USA Today*
Bestselling Author

Build Hope: 40 Days with Nehemiah to Bless Your World is Biblical, thoughtful, enjoyable, and challenging. Grounded in Scripture, packed with insights, served with many stories, and then applied through questions and responses, you will benefit hugely from letting the Lord Jesus use this little book to grow hope in you for your place of mission.

—Alex Absalom, co-founder of Dandelion Resourcing and
The Naturally Supernatural Course

One of the messages of Nehemiah is how much you can accomplish when you align yourself with the will and plan of God. Nehemiah and his followers were able to do the impossible because they did what God called them to do. Michael Carey has proven you don't have to rebuild a wall to do the will of God. In his book, *"Build Hope - 40 Days with Nehemiah to Change Your World,"* Michael Carey gives us a panoramic view of the trials, tribulations, and triumphs of a man on a mission to restore not only the fallen walls, but the hope and faith of God's chosen people. Nehemiah sought God for direction and favor, he fasted and prayed, he made a plan - then he approached the king. This in-depth study of Nehemiah shows the reader how to be an overcomer in today's world of chaos, disease, destruction, and injustice. I highly recommend this book as a powerful and timely weapon in our battle to do justice for such a time as this.

—Bishop Merton Clark, Lead – Truth Revealed
International Ministries, Inc.

Michael Carey's *Build Hope* is an excellent resource to inspire our churches and organizations to live out vision like Nehemiah. I have known Michael for many years and have always admired how he led his congregation to grow steadily while "building hope" in a multitude of ways throughout the community. When I heard about Michael and Lynn's willingness to relocate into a disadvantaged neighborhood, I was inspired by their boldness to back up their beliefs with their behavior. That is so like Nehemiah. But more importantly, that is so like Christ. This practical, life application approach to Nehemiah's story could be formative for laypeople in their devotional life as well as life group studies.　　　　　　　　—Lead Pastor Mark Ragsdale, Church at Viera

Building Hope is a wonderful study for small groups or personal daily devotionals. Michael shares candidly both his positive and challenging experiences to help us understand both his walk with faith and Nehemiah's reliance on God's sovereign power to change people. I love the way he weaves in his and Lynn's personal stories and experiences along with Nehemiah's story of courage and hope. While Nehemiah was a wall builder, he was also a relationship/community builder which parallels Michael's efforts to build bridges through missional ministry. We learn from Nehemiah that great leaders require humility and grace to truly impact the people around them. I am grateful for this study and the impact it had on me and will have on so many others. I'm reminded that good is more powerful than evil and our greatest weapon for hope-building is prayer.　　—Dr. Tony Ferretti, Psychologist, Speaker, Author

I still remember Dr. Michael Carey's messages on Nehemiah. As he led us through Nehemiah's journey to rebuild ancient Jerusalem, I sensed God's call to run for office with the hope of restoring public trust in our city. How delightful it is that Dr. Carey made this in-depth teaching available to everyone to use in their own spiritual journey.

　　　　　　—Mark Brimer, PhD; former mayor of Satellite Beach, Florida

I followed Sister Irene Summerford as director of The DOCK afterschool ministry, so I was delighted to read your remembrance of her unrelenting faith. This book is also thought provoking and causes me to ponder over so many things I've faced on my life. Your questions that you told us to think and ponder were serious! This is an excellent study of Nehemiah!

　　　　　　—Botavia Jackson, former director of The Dorcas Outreach
Center for Kids

Build Hope offers a way for us moving through a time of exile separated recently by pandemic and witnesses to declining interest in church and faith to find hope and purpose as God›s people in our day, learning from Nehemiah.

　　　　　　—Rev. Dr. Paige M. McRight, retired as Executive Presbyter, Central
Florida; author

MICHAEL CAREY

BUILD HOPE

WILD
FAITH
PRESS

Build Hope
40 Days with Nehemiah to Bless Your World

Copyright © 2022 by Michael Carey
ISBN 978-0-578-86912-4

Published by WILD FAITH PRESS, Melbourne, Florida

WILD
FAITH
PRESS

Printed in the United States of America

DEDICATION

To Lynn,
my gracious and enduring partner in love, life, and ministry.

CONTENTS

ACKNOWLEDGEMENTS

To the fellow Jesus-followers who've called me "pastor," I'm forever honored by the privilege of leading our hope-building adventures.

I'm deeply grateful to friends whose ongoing encouragement and coaching were instrumental in birthing this book. John Krehbiel's support has been a tonic. My own hope-building has been sustained by twenty-five years of prayer-partnership with Jeff Hoy and Wally Schilling. Ongoing conversation with Jesse Alexander has catalyzed my disciple-making initatives.

Charles Brockwell and Lynn Brockwell-Carey reviewed my drafts and offered helpful suggestions. Wendy Stackable's skillful editing refined this work immeasurably.

To God be the glory! Nehemiah's declaration is also my own: "The joy of the Lord is my strength" (8:10).

BLESSED DISCONTENT!

Irene Summerford overflowed with joy, even as she endured a lifetime of poverty. Some of her neighbors staved off hunger by succumbing to crime, satisfying other people's appetites. But feasting upon the "Bread of Life" (John 6:35), Sister Irene became an apostle of hope. She gathered children on a tarp under an old oak tree and boiled hot dogs for them with a generator and crockpot. Irene captured their imaginations with singing puppets and lively Bible stories. Every child knew Sister Irene's "formula": "Jesus + School = Success." Though surrounded by despair, she was energized by irrepressible hope. Hardly a demure church lady, Irene would even in "get in the faces" of drug dealers, insisting that Jesus could redeem their lives, too.

I began to hear "Sister Irene stories" in the early 2000s. Parishioners from my congregation assisted with her sidewalk Sunday School, called Project Light. My wife Lynn became the director of a fledgling, faith-based neighborhood restoration organization. Following "Christian Community Development" principles, Lynn and her colleagues built relationships with residents who yearned for positive change and welcomed partnerships with well-resourced outsiders.

Irene's pioneering presence and contagious joy accelerated the neighborhood's revitalization. The sidewalk Sunday School became a five-day-a-week, after-school safe haven. Dozens of volunteers helped children with homework and taught them the scriptures. Within a few years, Lynn and Irene involved hundreds of diverse people in designing, funding, and constructing a beautiful home for this ministry. Inspired by Dorcas, the servant-hearted woman celebrated in Acts 9:36, Irene's vision became the Dorcas Outreach Center for Kids—The DOCK.

Our hearts broke when Irene succumbed to cancer just months before The DOCK was completed. A few hours before she died, I stood at her bedside and lamented that she wouldn't see it finished. Without opening her eyes, Irene whispered, "Pastor, I've already seen it."

More than a decade after her death, Irene's hope-building initiative prospers. The DOCK's parent organization—Neighbor Up Brevard—took possession of and demolished dilapidated, drug-ridden apartments across the street from the DOCK, replacing them with eighteen units of beautiful and affordable Key West-style apartments. In 2018, the DOCK Teen Center was constructed to accommodate scores of teenagers who had been nurtured in hope for as long as they could remember. These changes, combined with the positive influence of tenacious long-time residents and new Habitat for Humanity homeowners, transformed the Booker T. Washington Neighborhood of Melbourne, Florida, into a safe and enjoyable place to live. In 2015, Lynn and I made it our home.

This marvelous sequence of events began because Irene and her partners cultivated a *healthy and holy discontent*. Even as she overflowed with joy, Irene's huge impact emerged from her faithful stewardship of negative emotions.

Discontent is often viewed negatively, especially among Christians. An old Gospel song insists that because of Jesus, "Now I am happy all the day." Of course, discontent is unhealthy if we obsess on what we don't have or what we don't like about ourselves. Unhealthy discontent may plague us when we cross paths with people who are attractive, affluent, talented, or successful. We are especially vulnerable to unhealthy discontent when we see people who, with total disregard to God, enjoy comfortable, self-absorbed lives.

Discontent is also unhealthy when our emotions are controlled by things we cannot change. For good reason, the "Serenity Prayer," attributed to Reinhold Niebuhr, became a mantra for millions:

> God, grant me the serenity to accept the things I cannot change,
> Courage to change the things I can,
> And wisdom to know the difference.

Biblical witnesses declare that the Lord hears our lament, empathizes with our distress, and applies balm to our hearts and minds. After the psalmist admitted that "I was envious of the arrogant; I saw the prosperity of the wicked. For they have no pain," he discovered that "my flesh and my heart may fail, but God is the strength of my heart and my portion forever" (Psalm 73:3-4, 26). *God's steadfast love is our best tonic for unhealthy discontent.*

Divine love is fully manifested in Jesus Christ and mediated by God's indwelling Spirit. It frees us from anxiety and fills us with God's joy. While awaiting execution, the Apostle Paul declared:

> Rejoice in the Lord always; again I will say, Rejoice.

> ...I have learned to be content with whatever I have. I know what it is to have little, and I know what it is to have plenty. In any and all circumstances I have learned the secret of being well-fed and of going hungry, of having plenty and of being in need. I can do all things through him who strengthens me.   Philippians 4:4, 11b-13

God provides serenity for the things we cannot change. Yet scripture also teaches us that God gives us courage to deal with the discontent we have for things that *can* be changed. That's why I've written this book.

Discontent can be healthy. Sin and suffering were *not* God's intent. Seeing human brokenness stokes holy discontent within the heart of the Triune God. The overarching trajectory of God's self-revelation—from the burning bush to the crucified Christ, risen Lord, and Spirit-filled Church—conveys divine passion to redeem and restore creation. People drawn into a relationship with Jesus receive His grace and much more. God's indwelling Spirit also conveys the Father's passion for holiness and wholeness. *As partners in Christ's mission, God's holy discontent becomes ours.*

Do not ignore discontent. We must reject passivity when life disappoints. Discern whether discontent is unholy and unhealthy or holy and healthy. Faithfulness to God involves understanding your emotions. If you conclude that your discontent is unholy and unhealthy, pursue the path of healing. *But if you discern that its holy and healthy, invite God to make you a hope-builder.*

The Bible provides marvelous glimpses of how holy discontent can be channeled into blessing: Hope-building heroes include Moses and Miriam, David and Hezekiah, Paul, and Barnabas. Yet the most detailed account is the saga of Nehemiah, the Jewish cupbearer who left the Persian court to rebuild Jerusalem's walls and restore community. Nehemiah's story occurred long before Christ, but Nehemiah's odyssey provides practical steps for Christ-followers who embrace God's mission.

Many commentators have written about Nehemiah. This book complements previous commentaries in five ways.

1. ORDINARY HOPE-BUILDERS

Nehemiah's hope-building path is relevant for those who don't see themselves as leaders. These "Nehemiah briefings" can inspire and empower anyone to be a positive influence. Hope-building know-how is essential whenever Christ-followers sense the Holy Spirit leading them to start a Scout troop, initiate a neighborhood watch, organize a missional community, or run for city council. Nehemiah's path can be taken by anyone.

2. FEMALE HOPE-BUILDERS TOO!

Some streams of Christianity are ambivalent—even opposed—to female leadership. Yet we dare not forget Rahab, Deborah, Priscilla, Lydia, Phoebe, Junia, and of course, Irene's favorite—Dorcas—significant leaders, despite their patriarchal context.

3. MISSIONAL HOPE-BUILDERS

Nehemiah's odyssey can be especially helpful for missional Christ-followers, disciples who embody the prayer that "Your Kingdom come. Your will be done, on earth as it is in heaven" (Matthew 6:10). The key is to view

Nehemiah's wall-building in its context. In ancient times, city walls were crucial for security. Before a community could flourish, protection from marauders was essential. But the goal of following Jesus is "bridge-building," not "wall-building." As Paul declared, the news of Jesus' life, death, and resurrection is "the message of reconciliation" (2 Corinthians 5:19). Celebrating the reconciliation of Jews and Gentiles, Paul declared that "[Jesus] is our peace; in his flesh he has made both groups into one and has broken down the dividing wall, that is, the hostility between us" (Ephesians 2:14).

The first generation of Christians didn't build walls of protection from temptation and persecution. On the contrary, Jesus' disciples were sent into Jewish synagogues and into Greco-Roman culture as heralds of good news. How tragic that anxiety over Christendom's decline persuades many Christians to succumb to varied forms of "wall-building."

Disciples of Jesus cannot allow fears of secularism or cultural diversity to forge a siege mentality. God sends us to embody Jesus, even among his despisers, despite the risks. As with our apostolic role models—Paul and Barnabas or Priscilla and Aquila—our mission is to build relational bridges as bold heralds of good news. Paradoxically, Nehemiah the wall-builder provides great lessons about how to tear down dividing walls and build communities of hope.

4. FORTY-DAY ODYSSEY

In order to facilitate personal transformation, this commentary utilizes the forty-day format pioneered by Rick Warren.[1] As the Spirit led Jesus to set aside forty days to clarify his mission, we who follow Jesus would benefit from forty-day seasons of reflection. Engaging Nehemiah's journey for six weeks could be transformative. You could take this journey on your own. There could be greater impact if you make it with others. Reading and reflecting with a small group, a missional community, or your whole congregation would provide additional insights and mutual encouragement.

5. EYEWITNESS TESTIMONY

While drawing from lessons learned by other leaders, this labor of love shares glimpses of my own successes and failures as a leader striving to build hope. It also chronicles amazing developments that emerged from Lynn and Irene's hope-building partnership. These precious stories are my grateful testimony for what the Lord can do when ordinary disciples put their holy discontent into God's hands.

THE JOURNEY FROM DISCONTENT

One of my treasured childhood memories is the summer I helped my dad build our garage. Though employed in the space program, he was trained as a mechanical engineer. Dad loved hands-on projects. After becoming dissatisfied with a carport, he envisioned how to expand and enclose it. This do-it-yourself project introduced me to the wonderful world of hammers and nails. More profoundly, it transformed me into someone who takes great satisfaction in building something better. Whether assembling garden boxes, pounding nails for Habitat for Humanity, or organizing ministry teams, my joy soars because my dad drew me into his garage-shaped vision.

A marvelous dimension of God's immense love is His patient persistence in enlisting us in His hands-on mission to redeem this world. After Jesus completed His redemptive work, He commissioned His disciples to make disciples (Matthew 28:19). The rest of the New Testament attests to the amazing fulfillment of Jesus' prediction that "the one who believes in me will also do the works that I do and, in fact, will do greater works than these, because I am going to the Father" (John 14:12).

We were fashioned for greater things. According to the Apostle Paul, "we are God's workmanship, created in Christ Jesus to do good works" (Ephesians 2:10, CSB). God the Father created us, God the Son redeemed us, and God the Spirit empowers us. As you begin this forty-day journey with Nehemiah, invite the Lord to use this inspiring odyssey to help you undertake "greater things" than you ever imagined.

DAY 1

FACE EXILE

Obscure Old Testament stories can be incredibly relevant. As children, many of us learned about the patriarchs, the Exodus from Egypt, and kings like David. Yet the Jews' exile to Babylon and their return to the Promised Land provides rich insight and inspiration for our current-day situation. Before plunging into Nehemiah's story, let's get a grasp of his context.

In 586 B.C., the Babylonians conquered Judea. Many Jews were forced to relocate to present-day Iraq and Iran. Living in exile was tough. Often the Jews were taunted:

> By the rivers of Babylon—
>   there we sat down and there we wept
>   when we remembered Zion.
> On the willows there
>   we hung up our harps.
> For there our captors
>   asked us for songs,
> and our tormentors asked for mirth, saying,
>   "Sing us one of the songs of Zion!"
> How could we sing the Lord's song
>   in a foreign land?   Psalm 137:1-4

How painful, to live out your days in a place where your faith is mocked. Yet a prophet who journeyed with fellow Jews declared that God planned to utilize their suffering:

> Thus says the LORD of hosts, the God of Israel, to all the exiles whom I have sent into exile from Jerusalem to Babylon: Build houses and live in them; plant gardens and eat what they produce. Take wives and have sons and daughters; take wives for your sons, and give your daughters in marriage, that they may bear sons and daughters; multiply there, and do not decrease. But seek the welfare of the city where I have sent you into exile, and pray to the LORD on its behalf, for in its welfare you will find your welfare.   Jeremiah 29:4-7

This rosy view seems strange, until we understand God's purpose. *The Lord uses adversity to refine authentic faith.* Being sent out from the Promised Land required God's people to depend on God's provision.

The Lord also had a missional agenda. The Jews were sent to Babylon to advance God's mission on earth. By commanding them to settle in Babylon and co-exist with non-Jewish neighbors, God planned to use their proximity to further the "welfare" of a nation, even though that nation didn't share their beliefs or their values.

Might God have such plans for us?

OUR OWN "EXILE"

In the past, an overwhelming percentage of Europeans and Americans embraced a Judeo-Christian worldview, fostering a culture often called "Christendom," not that Christianity was fully practiced. Christians often cherry-picked aspects of Jesus' teaching while ignoring the rest. While sincere in their devotion, many disciples of Jesus practiced a reduced, culturally conditioned Christianity.[2]

When Christendom prevailed, identifying as a Christian was comfortable. Government entities propagated aspects of Christian teaching. Public school teachers taught Bible lessons and led children in prayer. Media outlets self-censored sexual immorality from their programs. Clergymen frequently appeared on "Most Admired" lists. Churches were often full.

Christendom isn't dead. In some parts of the United States, its decline has just begun. Yet it's undeniable that practicing Christians are shrinking from the majority to the minority of the population. Immigration isn't the cause—Christian Hispanic immigrants actually outnumber Muslim, Hindu, and Buddhist immigrants. The primary factor is the decline in the percentage of Americans who no longer claim to be religious. 26 percent of the population now identifies as "Nones" (no religious inclination), including 40 percent of Millennials.[3]

To American Christians old enough to remember the dominance of Christendom, this decline brings a sense of loss. Even though we remain the largest religious group, it was more comfortable to be in the majority. The U.S. Constitution still protects religious freedom, yet it's unpleasant when non-Christians openly disagree or mock our beliefs. Occasionally, Christ-followers experience discrimination.[4] By far, the most frustrating issue is the experience of losing cultural dominance. It's a new kind of exile. Without leaving, people of faith increasingly feel like strangers in their homeland.

Unlike the Jewish captivity of the Old Testament, our experience of exile isn't imposed by a conqueror. We've been losing majority status because fewer people choose to practice Christianity. This decline started long ago. In recent decades, it's accelerated. After the Enlightenment and the Scientific Revolution launched the modern era, secular worldviews began to challenge church teaching. Yet Christendom's worst injuries have been self-inflicted. As "Christian nations" engaged in wars of conquest, persecution of Jews, crusades against Muslims, colonization of non-Europeans, enslavement of Africans, genocide of native peoples, and economic exploitation of the poor, the good news of Jesus has been obscured.

Furthermore, the church failed to follow in the footsteps of its founder. Instead of practicing self-sacrifice for others, the institutional church often seems focused on self-preservation. Instead of making disciples who live like Jesus, church rituals have prioritized "sin-management."[5]

Christians must face the brutal facts. Our cultural exile is largely due to the failures of the "faithful." It will surely accelerate unless we choose to embody Jesus' grace and truth.

HOPE IN EXILE

Christianity as a movement will *not* die because of cultural exile. Quite the contrary, in God's hands, loss of status can forge authentic faith. The faithfulness of the persecuted believers in Asia reminds us to depend solely on God, which will revive the church. During the most oppressive years of Maoist totalitarianism, the underground church prospered in China. In the most secular parts of Western Europe, new expressions of church are emerging. How the American church responds to its decline could foster a restoration of genuine Christian practice.

The key is overcoming fear, for fear makes people ungracious. Fear of secularism prompts many Christians to vote exclusively for politicians simply because they promise to restore their cultural prominence. Fear can distort our posture towards neighbors. If we minimize contact with non-believers, we reduce our influence. *Christian fearfulness actually accelerates secularism.*

Jesus said, "Do not let your hearts be troubled, and do not let them be afraid" (John 14:27). To help us face our fears, the scripture provides remarkable role models. Many champions lived during the period of exile: Jeremiah, Daniel, Shadrach, Meshach, Abednego, Esther, and Ezra. Each hero's story demonstrates an aspect of how God's people can thrive in the minority. Indeed, the exile forged strong faith. Many Jews became more faithful in Babylon than their ancestors had been in the Promised Land.

With faith-forged people, God inaugurated a plan to rebuild Judea. In 539 BC, a "new sheriff" took charge of the Middle East. King Cyrus of Persia defeated the Babylonians and conquered their empire. Amazingly, this idol-worshipping monarch became God's instrument:

Thus says the LORD…
who says of Jerusalem, "It shall be inhabited,"

and of the cities of Judah, "They shall be rebuilt,
   and I will raise up their ruins"…
who says of Cyrus, "He is my shepherd,
   and he shall carry out all my purpose";
and who says of Jerusalem, "It shall be rebuilt,"
   and of the temple, "Your foundation shall be laid."

Isaiah 44:24, 26b, 28

Sponsored by Cyrus, caravans of Jews made the long journey to resettle and rebuild Jerusalem.[6] However, the city's walls remained in rubble. In the ancient world, fortified walls were a necessary defense against local marauders and foreign invaders. Elaborate gates containing multiple stalls allowed business to be transacted while preventing strangers from entering the city. Despite efforts to rebuild, an unrepaired wall kept the holy city vulnerable.

The situation seemed hopeless, until a Jew in exile "sat down and wept" (Nehemiah 1:4). How he faced his discontent will help us build hope…despite our "exile."

QUESTIONS TO PONDER:

1. Which heroes from the time of Jewish exile have you found inspirational?
2. Have you noticed the decline of Christendom culture? How does it make you feel?
3. How could adapting to our cultural exile deepen and strengthen us as Christ-followers?
4. How could churches better demonstrate authentic Christianity?

DAY 2

HEALTHY AND HOLY DISCONTENT

God's people may have had good reason to be unhappy. Bad news from Jerusalem broke Nehemiah's heart:

> The words of Nehemiah son of Hacaliah. In the month of Chislev, in the twentieth year, while I was in Susa the capital, one of my brothers, Hanani, came with certain men from Judah; and I asked them about the Jews that survived, those who had escaped the captivity, and about Jerusalem. They replied, "The survivors there in the province who escaped captivity are in great trouble and shame; the wall of Jerusalem is broken down, and its gates have been destroyed by fire."

> When I heard these words I sat down and wept, and mourned for days, fasting and praying before the God of heaven.
> Nehemiah 1:1-4

As far as we know, Nehemiah had never seen the holy city of Jerusalem. But as a Jew growing up in a foreign land, he was immersed in the memories of previous generations:

Many Jews-in-exile would not forget the holy city. *Their devotion to the one true God actually grew deeper.* As one Jew wrote:

> If I forget you, O Jerusalem,
>   let my right hand wither!
> Let my tongue cling to the roof of my mouth,
>   if I do not remember you.
> Psalm 137:5-6

Nor did they weaken in their commitment to Judaism. Rather than bring Babylonian and Persian idols into their homes, many Jews shared their faith with the generation born into exile. Seventy years later, the Persian conquest of the Babylonians provided their descendants the opportunity to return. Thousands of devoted Jews gave up the security and familiarity of Mesopotamia to resettle their ancestral homeland.

NEHEMIAH'S DISCONTENT

Nehemiah's ancestors didn't accompany the initial returnees. He enjoyed a privileged life in the Persian palace, the "citadel of Susa." At the end of chapter one, we discover a stunning facet of Nehemiah's life—he was "cupbearer to the king" (Neh. 1:11). Though a member of a conquered minority, Nehemiah rose to a prestigious position: he served wine to King Artaxerxes, the grandson of Cyrus. Nehemiah was well-paid, well-dressed, and well-housed. Though a servant, his proximity to the king gave him great status. He overheard palace intrigues. Perhaps the king asked his counsel. No wonder he hadn't ventured to the "wild west."

But despite his Persian entrenchment, the Jewish cupbearer thought often of Jerusalem. Perhaps he dreamed of making a pilgrimage to worship in the recently rebuilt Temple. When his brother returned, Nehemiah eagerly inquired of the city's welfare.

Hanani's report changed Nehemiah's life: "Those who survived the exile and are back in the province are in great trouble and disgrace. The wall of Jerusalem is broken down, and its gates have been burned with fire" (1:3). Nehemiah was inconsolable: "I sat down and wept. For some days, I mourned and fasted and prayed before the God of heaven" (1:4).

Nehemiah's discontent was healthy. He wept for good reason. God's people—his people—faced great peril. Broken walls and burned gates left returning Jews vulnerable to attack. Nehemiah's discontent was holy. It expressed God's passion for the Jews' well-being.

YOUR DISCONTENT

The sources of our discontent are many. Discontent can be unhealthy, the fruit of wounds and bitterness. Discontent can be unholy. It certainly doesn't express God's concern if your unhappiness is due to sin or your devotion to an idol. Unhealthy discontent necessitates emotional healing, perhaps with the help of a counselor. Unholy discontent can only be remedied with repentance.

Yet there are numerous reasons for us to have healthy and holy discontent. Are you deeply concerned for your neighborhood? Your city? Your country? How about the state of our world? Are you troubled by the plight of refugees? Does human trafficking break your heart? Are you haunted by images of starving people? Are you concerned for the spirit of bitterness and alienation in our own country? Do you feel burdened by people who don't know Jesus? What about the state of the Church? Is your own congregation effective in God's mission?

It's not healthy to feel deep discontent over everything. Yet God gives everyone a particular burden for a cause that can't be ignored.

MY DISCONTENT

Several decades ago, I was overcome with holy discontent as a pastor. A year previous, I had moved from a smaller congregation to a larger one. There was much to appreciate about my new parish—a beautiful beachside community populated by high-tech workers. Neither a retirement haven nor a tourist trap, its multi-generational demographics were unusual for coastal Florida. The congregation was strong. I followed a successful pastorate. My family and I were warmly welcomed. What's not to like?

Yet in this ideal setting, I soon experienced discontent. While privileged to lead many sincere Christ-followers, there were obvious signs of spiritual shallowness. Discipleship ministries were weak, giving by the affluent seemed paltry, and few volunteers served with local mission partners. Other than attracting people to worship services, the church seemed to have marginal influence. This ineffectiveness was apparent as we tracked the participation of new members. If thirty newcomers joined the church, ten seemed to disappear within a few months and ten more merely lingered at the margins of congregational life. Perhaps ten of the original thirty became active in Christian community. While .333 is a great batting average in baseball, it was discouraging to impact only a third of our new members. Much more than baseball was at stake.

Jim Collins wrote that a key step in organizational health is for leaders to "face the brutal facts."[7] Instead of making excuses for malaise, the Holy Spirit cultivated my passion and courage. After I named our weaknesses to the church's elders, we agreed to search for remedies. Seeking insights from pastors of effective churches, my associate pastor colleague and I discovered the purpose-driven approach popularized by Rick Warren, pastor of Saddleback Community Church. This seemed biblical, workable, and adaptable to my congregation's core values.

Within months we sat amidst a vast crowd in California. The Purpose Driven Church Conference was a watershed. We gained insights and learned techniques that would transform our congregation. Yet the key event was an epiphany in a bathroom!

BATHROOM BARKERS

Between sessions, most of the three thousand attendees would make a beeline for the restrooms. I found myself in a line that stretched far outside the men's room door. To my relief, it moved quickly because Saddleback Church had bathroom "barkers!" Cheerful voices rang out: "This stall is free!" or "Space available, no reservation required!" Positioned before the long row of toilets were four ushers who insured that each was utilized efficiently.

Assuming that these men were Saddleback staff, I declared, "Whatever they pay you guys is not enough." One replied, "Ha, you couldn't pay me to do this. I'm an accountant. I serve on the Bathroom Hospitality Team. I took paid leave to help with this conference."

Suddenly, bright hope pierced my holy discontent. If the purpose-driven model could change self-centered suburbanites into selfless volunteers who served in smelly bathrooms, our search was over. Becoming "purpose-driven Presbyterians" became our motivating vision, providing me and my colleagues with energy, courage, and the insights needed to make costly (even controversial) changes that led to positive change. On many levels, the quality and scope of our church's ministry increased dramatically. Within four years we launched our own annual Purpose-Driven Presbyterians Conference. Over the next seven years, two thousand pastors and lay leaders with holy discontent journeyed to see what God was doing in Satellite Beach.

In the decades since, I've ridden other waves of holy discontent. We're not to obsess over everything that needs improving. While every broken place in creation matters to God, it's unhealthy for mortals to attempt to shoulder all the world's problems. As bearers of the Holy Spirit, neither can we ignore the world's brokenness. *God's passion to bring His Kingdom to earth makes Jesus' disciples passionate for some specific cause and corner of God's world.* We can trust our gracious Lord to help us discern where its best to invest our energies. God doesn't want to burden us with more than we can bear.

The key is learning to heed the Holy Spirit's leadings, so we focus our attention on a realistic set of challenges. Spiritual discernment is our first step in striving to embody God's holy passion in a healthy way.

Areas of Discontent	Seems Holy or Unholy?	Seems Healthy or Unhealthy?
1)		
2)		
3)		
4)		
5)		
6)		
7)		

QUESTIONS TO PONDER:

Take time to reflect on the areas of greatest discontent in your own life. Use the space provided to record your discernment. In the days to come, there will be opportunity to consider your next steps.

DAY 3

PRAY AUTHENTICALLY

Hope emerges when bad news prompts us to pray. The dismal report on the state of Jerusalem that came from Nehemiah's brother devastated Nehemiah:

> When I heard these words I sat down and wept, and mourned for days, fasting and praying before the God of heaven.   Nehemiah 1:4

Authentic prayer often emerges from deep sadness. Nehemiah mourned as if a loved one had died. He grieved intensely because he cared passionately for Zion, the epicenter of God's reign.

THE POWER OF PRAISE

Initially, Nehemiah couldn't eat because of grief. He continued his fast as a discipline. Food deprivation accentuated his spiritual awareness. He sat in silence, speechless because he felt powerless. Eventually, he embraced the Jewish pathway to empowerment—praise and confession:

> I said, "O LORD God of heaven, the great and awesome God who keeps covenant and steadfast love with those who love him and keep his commandments; let your ear be attentive and your eyes open to hear the prayer of your servant that I now pray before you day and night for your servants, the people of Israel, confessing the sins of the people of Israel, which we have sinned against you. Both I and my family have sinned.   Nehemiah 1:5-7

Nehemiah opened his mouth to pray because "the great and awesome God" is ready and able to deal with our discontent. Nothing is too broken or too damaged for God's redemptive love.

He began by praising the Lord's faithfulness. Nehemiah recalled the deliverance of the Hebrew slaves from Egypt and the exodus of exiled Jews from Mesopotamia. He remembered that God "keeps covenant and steadfast love with those who love him and keep his commandments."

Genuine prayer is grounded in praising the One whose name was revealed to Moses in a burning bush. Yahweh is often translated "the LORD." It's a mysterious name, literally meaning ""I AM WHO I AM"" (Exodus 3:14). The true God transcends space, time, and human expectations. Our hope is based on the sovereign freedom of the One who "abounds in steadfast love" (Exodus

34:6, NRSV). That's why Jesus taught his disciples to pray, "Our Father in heaven, hallowed be your name" (Matthew 6:9). Praising God's unfathomable love and transcendent power stokes our hope.

MOVING FROM GRIEF TO PRAISE

As you pray over your discontent, seek to move from grief into praise. Don't rush into a litany of needs. Recall who God is and what God has already done. If you struggle to find the words, remember how we praise people—we announce their noteworthy qualities:

> You have a beautiful smile!"
> You are a great mom!
> You are incredibly effective in motivating your staff!

We know how to praise people (and should praise them often). Praising God is similar. It's a learned behavior that becomes second nature with practice. Recall the hymns and praise choruses you've sung in worship. This classic hymn begins by celebrating the Creator:

> O Lord my God, when I in awesome wonder
> Consider all the works thy hands hath made,
> I see the stars, I hear the rolling thunder,
> Thy power throughout the universe displayed!
> Then sings my soul, my Savior God to thee,
> How great thou art! how great thou art!

The third verse draws us into praising God's redemptive love:

> And when I think of that God, his Son not sparing,
> Sent him to die, I scarce can take it in;
> That on the cross, my burden gladly bearing,
> He bled and died, to take away my sin.
> Then sings my soul, my Savior God to thee,
> How great thou art! How great thou art![8]

Singing or saying the songs you already know will strengthen your prayer life. Close the bedroom door, center yourself in silence, then sing God's praise. Take a hike in wilderness terrain where nobody but the Lord can hear you say it or sing it.

The Book of Psalms is our God-given resource for strengthening our praise-potential. The rest of scripture is God's Word spoken to people. God speaks through the Psalms as we listen to the heart-felt words that ancient people offered to God. Many psalms are pure praise. Other psalms intersperse praise with appeals for deliverance. Claim them as your words as you pray:

O LORD, our Sovereign, how majestic is your name in all the earth!
You have set your glory above the heavens.
Out of the mouths of babes and infants you have founded a bulwark
because of your foes, to silence the enemy and the avenger.

When I look at your heavens, the work of your fingers,
the moon and the stars that you have established;
what are human beings that you are mindful of them,
mortals that you care for them?
Yet you have made them a little lower than God,
and crowned them with glory and honor.   Psalm 8:1-5

I waited patiently for the LORD,
and he turned to me and heard my cry for help.
He brought me up from a desolate pit,
out of the muddy clay,
and set my feet on a rock,
making my steps secure.
He put a new song in my mouth,
a hymn of praise to our God.
Many will see and fear,
and they will trust in the LORD.   Psalm 40:1-3, CSB

AN UNSPOKEN QUESTION

Perhaps you have wondered, "Why would God want my praise? Is God vain?"

If you've pondered such unorthodox thoughts, you aren't alone. Be assured, God isn't vain. God doesn't need our praise. God is holy, all-powerful, all-knowing. God desires our praise because *we matter to God*. And God wants you to enjoy the benefit of praise. As C.S. Lewis explains, offering praise "completes your enjoyment":

> But the most obvious fact about praise—whether of God or anything—strangely escaped me. I thought of it in terms of compliment, approval, or the giving of honor. I had never noticed that all enjoyment spontaneously overflows into praise...The world rings with praise—lovers praising their mistresses, readers their favorite poet, walkers praising the countryside, players praising their favorite game...I think we delight to praise what we enjoy because the praise not merely expresses but completes the enjoyment; it is its appointed consummation.[9]

Enjoy God by offering your heart-felt praise.

POSITIONED BY CONFESSION

After praise comes supplication and intercession—praying for ourselves and others. Nehemiah spoke with humility and reverence: "let your ear be attentive and your eyes open to hear the prayer of your servant that I now pray before you day and night for your servants, the people of Israel, confessing the sins of the people of Israel, which we have sinned against you" (Neh. 1:6). With candor, he acknowledged that his people didn't deserve the Lord's benevolence: "We have offended you deeply, failing to keep the commandments, the statutes, and the ordinances that you commanded your servant Moses" (1:7).

Praise is rightly followed by confession of sin. If you are in Christ, the Lord has already forgiven you. Yet like praise, confession is fitting and therapeutic, as in our relationships with people. When we have said or done something that hurts another, naming it as sin and asking for forgiveness expresses love and faithfulness. Confessing sin initiates the removal of relational barriers. Forgiveness completes the removal.

Nehemiah's prayer of confession in 1:6-7 was generic, a sweeping acknowledgement of his and his people's unfaithfulness. Likely he also named specific offenses. As you move from praise into confession, ask the indwelling Spirit to make you aware of unconfessed sin. Perhaps your discontent has been fueled by guilt over complicity with evil. Maybe you've averted your eyes from injustice as idols captivated your attention. Acknowledge your sin to God. If you've hurt others, ask for their forgiveness. For encouragement reflect on Psalm 51, Colossians 3:21-14, and James 5:16.

To discern whether your discontent is holy and healthy, ask the Holy Spirit to search your heart for hidden sin or festering bitterness. Toxicity indicates that discontent is neither healthy nor holy. Confessing sin and seeking reconciliation with others will facilitate healing. *Only a healthy and whole child of God can be useful to our Lord.* As Augustine of Hippo wrote: "The confession of evil works is the first beginning of good works."[10]

QUESTIONS TO PONDER:

1. Do you have a time and place dedicated to daily prayer?
2. How could praise and confession strengthen your personal prayer life?
3. Have you named your discontent to God?
4. Do you sense how God wants to channel your discontent into positive action?

DAY 4

PRAY BOLDLY

Prayer changes us. Ever since his brother conveyed the dismal news of Jerusalem's weakness, Nehemiah wrestled with a gnawing sense that he should act. Crazy possibilities flooded his consciousness. But how could Nehemiah know whether his wild ideas were the Lord's leadings or his own delusions? Eventually, he realized that to discover their source, he would have to step out in faith. Nehemiah's prayer shifted into a bold dialogue:

> "Remember the word that you commanded your servant Moses, 'If you are unfaithful, I will scatter you among the peoples; but if you return to me and keep my commandments and do them, though your outcasts are under the farthest skies, I will gather them from there and bring them to the place at which I have chosen to establish my name.'"
> Nehemiah 1:8-9

REMIND GOD?

Nehemiah's words seem presumptive. Remind God what God said? Yet our Heavenly Father enjoys hearing His children recount His promises. As Tim Challies wrote,

> God loves to hear his own words prayed back to him! When a small child crawls up on the lap of their father and says, "Daddy when are you going to take us to the zoo like you promised?" the father smiles and assures his child he has not forgotten and is very much looking forward to doing what he promised (when the time is right). In the same way, our heavenly Father delights to hear us remind him of his promises to us.[11]

The Lord is pleased to hear us recount what is promised in scripture. God wants to entrust us with influence and resources as we pursue his mission. As Jesus declared, "Don't be afraid, little flock, because your Father delights to give you the kingdom" (Luke 12:32, CSB).

Many biblical characters claimed God's promises in prayer, including Jacob (Genesis 31:12), Moses (Exodus 32:11-14), Solomon (2 Chronicles 1:9), Daniel (9:15-16), and the Apostles (Acts 4:24-31). Preparing to ask God to send him back, Nehemiah remembered Jeremiah's assertion of God's promise to return Jews from exile:

Set up road markers for yourself,
  make yourself signposts;
consider well the highway,
  the road by which you went.
Return, O virgin Israel,
  return to these your cities.   Jeremiah 31:21

God could be trusted to fulfill the promise that the Jews would return and rebuild. But would Nehemiah be the leader to supervise the construction? God might have other plans. Perhaps God would raise up a different leader. Either way, Nehemiah could trust God to deal with his holy discontent. As the Apostle Paul testified: "I know how to make do with little, and I know how to make do with a lot. In any and all circumstances I have learned the secret of being content...I am able to do all things through him who strengthens me" (Philippians 4:12b, 13, CSB). The fulfilment of God's purposes (not our need for significance) yields the deepest joy.

GOD'S PROMISES

Rebuilding Jerusalem's walls wouldn't only fortify a vulnerable population. Restoring Zion would serve a far greater plan. As the Lord declared to Isaiah 300 years prior to Nehemiah's generation:

"It is too light a thing that you should be my servant
  to raise up the tribes of Jacob
  and to restore the survivors of Israel;
I will give you as a light to the nations,
  that my salvation may reach to the end of the earth."   Isaiah 49:6

Five hundred years later, God used the restored tribes of Jacob to give the world a Savior. Salvation became accessible to everyone. *Therefore we continue to pray bold prayers, claiming God's promises*:

- That neighbors who put their faith in Jesus will receive eternal life (Acts 2:38-39)
- That God will provide for our needs as we pray for "daily bread," for we are "of much more value" than "the birds of the air" whom "our heavenly Father feeds" (Matthew 6:11, 26)
- That as we "strive first for the kingdom of God and his righteousness....all these [necessities] will be given...as well" (Matthew 6:33)
- That the Lord will never forsake us, despite trial, shortage, and death (Romans 8:37-39)

+ That regarding spiritual growth, Jesus meant what he said when he declared: "Ask, and it will be given you" and "Give, and it will be given to you" (Matthew 7:7, Luke 6:38)
+ That that Spirit will cultivate the "fruit of...love, joy, peace, patience, kindness, generosity, faithfulness, gentleness, self-control" (Galatians 5:22-23)
+ That we are promised power to advance God's reign. As Jesus declared, "You will receive power when the Holy Spirit comes on you; and you will be my witnesses..." (Acts 1:8)

Notice the interwoven relationship between God's promises and our endeavors. Building hope requires human exertion, but our efforts reflect God's plans, God's promises, and God's power. We don't build on our own, for we are God's workmanship, created in Christ Jesus to do good works" (Ephesians 2:10, CSB). The Apostle also celebrated that "According to God's grace that was given to me, I have laid a foundation as a skilled master builder, and another builds on it. But each one is to be careful how he builds on it" (1 Corinthians 3:10, CSB).

AUDACIOUS PRAYER

Boldly claim God's promises, for "to live in His will makes us dangerous."[12] Dare to believe that the Lord will use you to threaten evil.

In 2001, a group of leaders asked my wife Lynn to direct a newly formed Christian community development organization, Neighbor Up Brevard, at that time called Brevard Neighborhood Development Coalition.[13] Isaiah 58:12 provided Neighbor Up Brevard's motivating vision: "you shall be called...the restorer of streets to live in." Lynn and the Board of Directors initially partnered with resident leaders in a small, historic community that had experienced dramatic change. What had once been a pleasant, tight-knit working class neighborhood had become the city's densest area of poverty and a haven for drug dealers and prostitutes. To express their restoration aspiration, its law-abiding residents petitioned the city to name it the Booker T. Washington Neighborhood, for the slave-turned-educator who championed learning, character formation, personal discipline, and the virtue of hard work.

At first, Neighbor Up Brevard organized community beautification projects. Friendships were spawned as volunteers and residents worked side by side. Efforts were made to listen to the expressed needs of the community. When the children of Booker T. Washington shared that they longed for "a place we can go after school and get help with our homework," Neighbor Up Brevard's leaders were inspired. They asked God for a leader. Long-time resident Irene Summerford was God's answer. Her holy discontent already manifested the sidewalk ministry that fed hungry children with hot dogs and Bible stories. Under Irene's leadership, a handful of volunteers transformed a vacant public housing apartment into a haven for childhood empowerment.

When this outreach outgrew its space, Lynn led the effort to build it a permanent home. She found only one lot with an owner willing to sell. It was beautiful, a live oak hammock in the heart of the community. When Irene heard this news, she exclaimed, "I've been claiming that lot in prayer for decades! I've been pleading with the Lord to preserve it for the children."

The vision was daunting. Neighbor Up Brevard was a fledgling organization. The $10,000 purchase price seemed unreachable. Lynn and I discussed whether to loan Neighbor Up Brevard the needed amount from our daughters' college funds. About that time, a Christian couple discovered this opportunity. The Lord led them to donate a tithe from an unexpected business windfall, providing the needed $10,000.

The Board of Directors initially planned to relocate old portable classrooms to house the program. Thoughtful and prayerful discussion convinced them that such an approach was inadequate. Despite not knowing how God would provide, a bold plan to construct a 3500 square foot facility emerged. Two years and $470,000 later, the Dorcas Outreach Center for Kids (The DOCK) was dedicated.

When people with holy discontent have the faith to pray bold prayers, God hears and acts. Often, God moves in surprising ways, enabling disciples to build hope. As the saying goes, "When God gives vision, God *also* gives provision." Countless churches, parachurch ministries, and humanitarian non-profit organizations do God's work because people with holy discontent discern God's vision and pray with boldness.

We are never guaranteed success. What we are promised is God's "favor," when we pray boldly to fulfill God's purposes. *Claim God's promises.*

QUESTIONS TO PONDER:

1. What scripture-based promises can you claim as you pray?
2. Does discerning and doing God's will guarantee physical safety?
3. How might discerning and doing God's will make you dangerous to evil?
4. Have you ever prayed boldly and been amazed at God's provision?

DAY 5

PRAY COURAGEOUSLY

God's people pray about the present while remembering the past. After recalling God's promises, Nehemiah appealed to God's faithfulness:

> They are your servants and your people, whom you redeemed by your great power and your strong hand. O Lord, let your ear be attentive to the prayer of your servant, and to the prayer of your servants who delight in revering your name. Give success to your servant today, and grant him mercy in the sight of this man!"

At the time, I was cupbearer to the king.   Nehemiah 1:10-11

Initially, Nehemiah spoke of God's people in third person: "They are your servants and your people, whom you redeemed...." Then he highlighted himself: "Lord, let your ear be attentive to the prayer of your servant." Despite serving in the Persian court, Nehemiah counted himself among faithful Jews "who delight in revering your name." Twice calling himself a "servant," Nehemiah declared his availability to God. His actions would match his words.

Through deep prayer, an audacious plan emerged, a project too big for Nehemiah to accomplish on his own. Taking a deep breath, Nehemiah's first "ask" was to appeal to God to use "your great power and your strong hand" to persuade a certain someone to sponsor Nehemiah's mission: "Give success to your servant today by granting him mercy in the sight of this man."

So, who was "this man"? Who else but Emperor Artaxerxes of Persia, for as the narrative announced, Nehemiah "was cupbearer to the king." As with Esther a generation before, of Nehemiah it could also be asked, "Who knows, perhaps you have come to your royal position for such a time as this" (Esther 4:14b, CSB). By providing a high position to Nehemiah, the Lord would provide the resources necessary to rebuild Jerusalem...if Nehemiah asked...and if Artaxerxes responded with "favor."

RISK READINESS

To leverage his position was dangerous. Nehemiah was accustomed to risk. Cupbearers served as poison detectors. Decades prior, Artaxerxes' father (Xerxes, the "god-king" invader of the movie 300) was poisoned by a member of the royal court. Cupbearers tasted risk every day.

Acting upon holy discontent would magnify the risks. Speaking about the sad state of Jerusalem might annoy Artaxerxes. No wonder Nehemiah fasted and prayed. Servants didn't discuss geopolitical issues with a monarch unless the king initiated the conversation. It was highly unusual for a servant to lobby.

Authentic prayer involves a willingness to take risks. Saying "yes" to God's call takes us into the unknown. We can't be sure that our plans will succeed. We could end up in situations feeling "over our heads." We risk our hearts being broken as we become intertwined in messy lives. We risk personality conflicts whenever we form mission teams that will take on daunting challenges. Perhaps our calling will risk our health and safety. Risk is an undeniable aspect of hope-building, yet faithful servants trust the one who promised: "I am with you always, to the very end of the age" (Matthew 28:20).

COMMITMENT RISK

There is also the risk inherent in commitment. Once you put your hand to the plow, you must focus on the work to which God has called you—at the risk of missing alluring opportunities. At the same Saddleback conference where I encountered the "bathroom barkers," Rick Warren taught me that to lead positive change, pastors must embrace commitment. Here's my recollection of his talk:

Time to tell you pastors what you don't want to hear. Write this in your notebook, "To lead a purpose-driven church, I will commit to remaining where God has planted me for at least five years" (3000 pastors gasped).

Maybe you're tempted to "climb the pastor-ladder." If so, you would be motivate to implement just enough change to yield sufficient successes to enhance your resume.

If you get the opportunity to move, you will likely announce that "God has called me to a new place." How can you be so sure? God may want you to commit to the transformation of a stagnant, complacent congregation, even if it takes years.

Laypeople are unlikely to "kill sacred cows" and restructure their congregations unless the pastor commits to implementing changes. Wouldn't it be better to assume that God wants you to "grow where you are planted," unless it's absolutely clear that your work is done, and that God is calling you elsewhere?"[14]

The auditorium was full of pensive faces. Rick had nailed it. *For God to harness our holy discontent for His purposes, we must be willing to embrace the risks that comes with commitment.*

I took the lesson to heart. My prayers for God's direction were repeatedly met with compelling signs that God wanted me to serve where I was planted. For seventeen more years, I poured myself into leading one church through a series of positive changes. In the process, God poured out favor. Staff and lay leaders devoted their time, talent, and treasure to the transformation of Trinity Presbyterian Church. Leaders searching for a more purposeful congregation were drawn to us. Many nominal believers who entered our community via worship services began spiritual journeys that transformed them into generous, committed servants of Jesus Christ. Within seven years, the congregation doubled in size and grew exponentially in its impact on the surrounding community.

Periodically Lynn and I re-examined our commitment to longevity. Each time, new growth opportunities in our leadership roles persuaded us that God wanted us to remain where we were planted.

There were benefits to staying rooted. We became influential in shaping a region that we loved. The best benefits were relational. Our children were grateful not to move during their teenage years. We enjoyed wonderful friendships and ever-widening partnerships. Staying rooted also brought risks.[15]

You must discern your own path. Holy discontent may lead to a commitment to invest yourself deeper in the community where you already reside. Or, like Nehemiah, holy discontent might cause you to move to a new community. Or perhaps the Lord will lead you to start an organization, plant a new church, launch a new business, or relocate your residence to an under-resourced neighborhood.

Be adventuresome. Pray with readiness.

QUESTIONS TO PONDER:

1. How might you become more available to God?
2. What risks do you face as you act upon holy discontent?
3. What benefits might you reap if you commit to God's calling?

DAY 6

EMBRACE SENT-NESS

God's people don't just *go* to worship. After gathering with God's people, we honor God by allowing ourselves to be *sent* as God's people into the world God loves.

Let's digest the rich insights we've gleaned from Nehemiah's first chapter. While historical, this saga transcends its setting. As we retrace the cupbearer's faith journey, we're each prompted to consider a new dimension of our own faith walk—my own "sent-ness." How might the Spirit use me to advance God's mission, wherever God wants?

Recall the disciples' first encounter with their resurrected Lord:

Having said this, he showed them his hands and his side. So the disciples rejoiced when they saw the Lord.

Jesus said to them again, "Peace be with you. As the Father has sent me, I also send you." After saying this, he breathed on them and said, "Receive the Holy Spirit." John 20:20-22 (CSB)

Jesus' crucifixion traumatized his followers. His ghastly, shameful death shattered their dreams. No wonder they were "overjoyed when they saw the Lord." Their hope had not been a delusion.

PEACE FROM HIS PRESENCE

Jesus greeted them with "Peace" and conveyed the calming confidence of his living presence. Whatever life brings, we never face challenges alone. We can *carpe diem* ("seize the day") because our resurrected Lord is powerfully present. As Paul testified from a prison cell:

Don't worry about anything, but in everything, through prayer and petition with thanksgiving, present your requests to God. And the peace of God, which surpasses all understanding, will guard your hearts and minds in Christ Jesus. Philippians 4:6-7 (CSB)

Unhealthy discontent need not consume you. Nor should healthy and holy discontent overwhelm you. The powerful presence of the risen Christ will "guard" your thoughts and feelings.

SENT DISCIPLES

Notice that we don't receive the peace of Christ by retreating from the world. Quite the contrary, Jesus bestows his peace as he sends us *into* the world: "Peace be with you. As the Father has sent me, I also send you." Jesus propelled the first disciples into mission even before his resurrection. Soon after they began to follow him, Jesus appointed seventy-two disciples and "sent them out two by two ahead of him to every town and place where he was to go" (Luke 10:1). Thrown into the work of teaching and healing, these "sent" disciples served as an advance team, intriguing people with works that provided a compelling foretaste of the coming Christ. After his resurrection, Jesus would send his disciples out much further—geographically and chronologically. Preparing to ascend to his Father, he promised to return as King of Kings and Lord of Lords. In the meantime, Jesus' mission is our mission. Our Lord sends us to advance God's reign in the world as disciples who make disciples:

> Go therefore and make disciples of all nations, baptizing them in the name of the Father and of the Son and of the Holy Spirit, and teaching them to obey everything that I have commanded you....
>
> Matthew 28:19-20a

Traditional translations of the original manuscripts render verse 19 as an imperative: "Go and make disciples." Yet the same Greek word for "go" (*poreunthentes*) can also be utilized as a present participle, and can be read: "As you go, disciple people..." (Matthew 28:19, ISV).

Perhaps Jesus intended two kinds of "go." Sent-ness can have different yet complementary meanings. Sent-ness can involve traveling to a new place to be a missionary. Yet Jesus' disciples also aspire to be missionaries if they remain where they are, "as they go" about their business. Some of the original disciples returned to their homes and made disciples in Jerusalem or surrounding region of Judea. The Holy Spirit sent others to Samaria, which was a hostile region for Jews. Some were sent to the "ends of the earth" (Acts 1:8). Within decades, clusters of disciples sprang up in distant regions of the Roman Empire: Asia Minor, Greece, Italy, Gaul, Spain, Egypt, Persia—even as far as India.

APOSTLE LEADERS

The Holy Spirit gives some of Jesus' disciples the spiritual gifts that enable them to lead other disciples in sent-ness. Jesus called them "apostles," for the Greek the word *apostolos* means "one who is sent".[16] Knowing that he needed to train leaders for his movement after he ascended to heaven, Jesus prayed throughout the night, then "he called his disciples and chose twelve of them, whom he also named apostles" (Luke 6:13). Eventually, this term was broadened to include other Spirit-anointed leaders whom Jesus sent as the vanguard of God's mission (Ephesians 4:11).

Sister Irene functioned as an apostle. Not only did she awaken disciples to their sent-ness in her "Jerusalem" (her own neighborhood), she also empowered disciples in her "Samaria" (more affluent areas where many DOCK volunteers and donors lived).

SENT NEAR OR FAR

Some Christ-followers discern God's call to relocate to another neighborhood, another region, or another nation. Other Christ-followers are sent to where they already live, work, and play. Either way, we are nowhere by accident. Wherever God calls, we are sent there to make disciples.

Until the 4th Century A.D., Jesus' disciples tended to see themselves as "sent people," even if they never went on a mission trip. This clarity was muddled after the Roman Empire adopted Christianity as its state religion. Rather than mentoring disciples to follow Jesus' lifestyle, Christian teaching focused on doctrines and rituals. Increasingly, God's mission was perceived as converting non-Christians in far-away places. This much-reduced religion produced many "Christians" who relished wars of conquest while embracing economic oppression, racism, colonialism, slavery, and the subjugation of women. Disgust towards this reduced and distorted Christianity eventually became an impetus to secularism.[17]

To restore the much-reduced Gospel and renew our awareness of sentness, missiologists (theologians who study mission) crafted a new word: *missional*. Adding "al" makes "mission" an adjective instead of a noun. Rather than the service of a few people in far-away places, a missional mindset underscores the reality that God's mission happens everywhere, all the time. Here's how a missional disciple might express his or her perspective:

> My surroundings are a mission field. My life is a never-ending mission trip. The reign of God will be more visible as I embody Jesus in daily life. The love of God will be evident as God uses me to bless others. As my life intrigues skeptical people, I will welcome the opportunity to share my faith.

We cannot sustain such lives on our own. We embrace this sent-ness because we are assured by Jesus' assurance of his powerful presence: "I am with you always, to the end of the age" (Matthew 28:20)... "You will receive power when the Holy Spirit has come upon you" (Acts 1:8).

Do you yearn to experience the Spirit's powerful presence? Invite Jesus to be your Lord. Give him command of your life. Continually ask him to heal your brokenness and re-form you in his image (Romans 12:2).

Cultivate habits that position you to hear and heed the Spirit's leadings. Each morning, ask the Spirit to open your eyes to opportunities to join the Lord in his mission to bless others. You will learn to recognize the Lord's "still small voice" (1 Kings 19:12, KJV). As you sense these "leadings," act in obedience, even if they interrupt your schedule. Seemingly insignificant actions can have powerful impact upon others.

JOANN'S SENT-NESS

JoAnn served for nearly a decade as a medical worker in an overwhelmingly Muslim country (not her actual name). She was motivated to go to North Africa not only from humanitarian concern; she also believed that God was sending her as a missionary. Each morning she prayed that her life and work would create opportunities to share the good news of Jesus. Because Christian mission work wasn't allowed in that country, spiritually significant conversations were low-keyed and discreet.

When JoAnn returned to the U.S., she didn't refer to herself as a former missionary, for she perceived that God was sending her to be a missionary in her hometown. After settling in her new home, JoAnn began to invite neighbors to tea. As relationships strengthened, she looked for the opportunities to engage in spiritually significant meaningful discussions. Before long, she was hosting micro-church gatherings for immediate neighbors and providing hospitality for international students from a nearby university.

Embrace your own sent-ness. *Whatever your circumstances, the Lord wants to harness your unique personality and capabilities to share grace and build hope in the world around you.* You can trust that wherever you are, you are sent "with power, for as Jesus said: "I am with you always" (Matthew 28:20). God's powerful presence is always at work: softening hard hearts, opening closed minds, awakening complacent disciples, and magnifying our modest efforts.

QUESTIONS TO PONDER:

1. What is "sent-ness" for Jesus-followers? What does it mean to "embrace sent-ness"? What are two very different expressions of sent-ness?
2. What is a "leading"? How might Christ-followers learn to recognize whether leadings are from the Holy Spirit?
3. Did reading about JoAnn's sent-ness intrigue you? How might you connect with your neighbors?

DAY 7

DISCERN SENT-NESS

Discerning *where* we are sent is a key issue for hope-builders. Aversion to commitment may tempt us to limit our altruism to "random acts of kindness." But to have significant impact, concentrate your attention on a particular place or group.

In discerning where, who, what, and how I should focus my energies, the scripture provides varied possibilities. One option is to focus on people who are already in your relational network, as Levi the tax collector did after he first followed Jesus:

> After this he went out and saw a tax collector named Levi, sitting at the tax booth; and he said to him, "Follow me." And he got up, left everything, and followed him.

> Then Levi gave a great banquet for him in his house; and there was a large crowd of tax collectors and others sitting at the table with them.   Luke 5:27-29

It's likely that you have influence in certain circles, especially among people with whom you work or play. Consider the possibility that God is sending you to share hope with people with whom you have a unique connection.

A missional focus could be on those who live near to you. In the Greek city of Thessalonica, "Jason's house" became a focal point for sharing God's grace. Jason graciously hosted the apostles and connected them to his neighbors. The apostles shared the news of God's grace in Jesus Christ (Acts 17:7). While this Gospel hospitality stirred up opposition, Paul described the Thessalonian church as "a model for all the believers" (1 Thessalonians 1:7, ISV).

Consider the possibility that the Lord is calling you to focus your missional energy on your immediate neighbors. In this lonely, individualistic culture, many people are starved for relationships, though they mask their hunger. Building bridges with neighbors through simple acts of hospitality can have a powerful impact. Shared meals, cookouts, children's playdates, and block parties are a mutual blessing.[18] A posture of hospitality can open closed minds and break open hard hearts as neighbors encounter the Spirit of Jesus in you.

Finally, the Holy Spirit could reveal God's call that you focus on people who live elsewhere, as when "Paul had a vision of a man of Macedonia standing and begging him, 'Come over to Macedonia to help us'" (Acts 16:9, ISV). Your "Macedonia" might be another part of town, another city, even another nation.

Jesus summarized these possibilities just before he ascended to heaven, telling his disciples that "you will receive power when the Holy Spirit has come upon you; and you will be my witnesses in Jerusalem, and in all Judea and Samaria, and to the ends of the earth" (Acts 1:8). For those initial disciples, "Jerusalem" represented their immediate surroundings and cultural sameness. "Judea" represented the wider geographic region that was culturally familiar. "Samaria" was a geographically close region with a different—even hostile—culture. Being sent to "the ends of the earth" would require the disciples to travel far distances and adapt to strange cultures. While the Lord sends disciples to all four types, individual disciples normally perceive God's call to one specific place at a time.

HOW TO DISCERN

Paul wrote to the Colossians that "we have not stopped praying for you and asking that you may be filled with the full knowledge of God's will with respect to all spiritual wisdom and understanding" (1:9b, ISV). Grasping this "knowledge...spiritual wisdom and understanding" begins with our perception of what we have called the Spirit's "leadings". We learn much of God's will from the scriptures and we also benefit from Spirit-given guidance.

To build hope effectively, you must discern where you are sent. This search for clarity begins as a private conversation between you and God. Invest time in personal Bible study, record your thoughts in a journal, and listen for the Spirit's leading in silent prayer (perhaps while fasting).[19] Hearing the Spirit's voice is easier when we retreat from daily distractions. Consider using church camp facilities, monastery guest houses, friends' vacation homes, or take hikes in desolate nature preserves. Get off the grid by turning off your phone.

After you have listened attentively to the Spirit's leadings, ask the Lord to confirm that you have heard correctly by sharing it with spiritually mature and trustworthy people. Pray also that the Lord will "open a door" that otherwise seem shut (Acts 14:27, 1 Corinthians 16:9). Or in the manner of Gideon, test your perception of God's will by setting out some kind of "fleece," asking God to orchestrate an unusual set of events that confirms your perception (Judges 6:36-40).

SENT TO BOOKER T. WASHINGTON?

After several years of leading Christian community development in the Booker T. Washington Neighborhood, Lynn sensed God's call to move our residence into the area. Her yearning wasn't surprising. John's Gospel reminds us that Jesus' redemptive pathway motivated him to "move into the neighborhood" (1:14, MSG). Inspired by Jesus, relocation into troubled neighborhoods is a common practice for Christ-followers who seek insight, credibility, and influence when they are called to catalyze community restoration.[20]

Yet, Lynn's sense of call was complicated by her family situation. At the time that she became Neighbor Up Brevard's executive director, she was married to the pastor of a large congregation and was mother to two young children. For a decade, Lynn commuted from an affluent, white, beachside community to an under-resourced, predominately African-American community on the mainland. This dichotomy would have crippled her effectiveness as a leader, if not for the friendship and grace offered by Irene Summerford and other community partners.

Seven years after Lynn began this work, I joined her at the Christian Community Development Conference (CCDA) in Miami and sat at the feet of pioneering leaders like John Perkins, Wayne Gordon, and Bob Lupton. I also began to wonder whether God was calling us to relocate. I wrestled with the prospect, not only because it would entail leaving our palm-covered paradise a block from the ocean. I had genuine concerns as to whether my congregation would accept its pastor moving his residence from their "Jerusalem" to their "Samaria." Lynn and my differing perspectives led to tensions between us. Two years later, while attending the CCDA Conference in Chicago, we got into such an intense discussion while riding the "L" that we missed our stop, requiring us to exit the train and wait for a return trip in a very distressed neighborhood. A sign?

Praying together, we asked God to clarify our sent-ness. Gradually, our circumstances began to favor relocation. We were empty-nesters and ready to downsize. Our congregation embraced a more missional vision that supported its pastor's relocation into a different kind of neighborhood.

During several days of prayer at a monastery, I began to envision our new home and grew excited at the prospect of designing it. Several months later, on a blustery winter's day of walking, talking, and praying on the barren terrain of the St. Sebastian River Preserve, Lynn and I covenanted with each other and the Lord to pursue building a home in the Booker T. Washington community. We both believed that we had heard God's voice, yet we also expected that God would confirm this call by overcoming obstacles and opening doors of opportunity. Over the next years, God knocked down barriers to our relocation in amazing ways:

1. We perceived the Spirit's leading to purchase a vacant lot on a particular corner, but it wasn't for sale. Habitat for Humanity owned the lot. After hearing of our vision, Habitat's director promised to sell us the lot. God provided the place!

2. Few homebuilders would be interested in constructing a smaller-than-normal house, and because of its location, we wouldn't be able to get a loan unless we found a contractor who would build the house at cost (no profit). Nonetheless, God provided such a builder.

3. Would a property appraisal yield a value at least equal to the cost of construction? This was critical so that we could get financing. Again, God provided—the appraisal came within $500 of the house construction cost.

4. Our builder discovered that the underground sewer and water lines were unfinished. The previous developer had abandoned work during the Great Recession. This lack of infrastructure seemed a showstopper. We prayed for a miracle. The next Sunday, that same developer walked into my congregation's lobby and asked me to lunch. You can be sure that I asked whether he could find paperwork that located the unfinished utility lines. Not only did he provide the key diagrams, he even met with building code officials to expedite the approval process. *God made a way, where there seemed to be no way.*

5. After all that drama, just as we were to take possession of the lot, the director of Habitat resigned. Habitat's Board of Directors decided to reconsider whether to sell us the lot. Lynn and I appeared before the Board and shared our vision. We faced some opposition, yet most of Habitat's Board embraced our vision of living in proximity with Habitat for Humanity partner families. They approved the sale, construction commenced, and in February 2015, we moved into our "dream house."

Once again, Lynn and I discovered the veracity of the adage: "When God gives vision, God gives provision". By overcoming the obstacles that nearly derailed our plans, God made it clear that we had correctly discerned our sent-ness.

Today, we live on a street full of young families living in homes that love built. We enjoy sharing life with our neighbors. Whether it's gathering for potluck dinners, swapping fishing advice, or chatting with the children as we pull weeds together in my garden, Lynn and I are richly blessed. Our God-given location provides wonderful opportunities to build hope.

Seek to discern where God sends you. Meditate on scripture and immerse yourself in prayer. As you sense God's leading, look for signs of God's confirmation.

Whether near or far, as missional disciples we are called to be missionaries *somewhere*. Most likely you will have the greatest impact in your "Jerusalem and Judea"—places where you live, work, and play.

Or like Lynn and me, you might be called to a "Samaria," a place that that is close geographically but very different from you culturally.

Or perhaps as a traditional missionary, you will be called somewhere that lies at "the ends of the earth."

Wherever God gives vision, God always gives provision!

QUESTIONS TO PONDER:

1. How does a Christ-follower position himself or herself to discern the Spirit's leading?
2. Have this week's readings given you more clarity about your own calling?
3. How could you listen more attentively for God's voice?
4. How might you get confirmation?

WEEK 2
Nehemiah 1:11-2:20

LEVERAGE INFLUENCE

Since childhood, I've been a dreamer. I've spend hours imagining buildings built, landscapes cultivated, and enterprises developed. I still have "brainstorms" that prompt me to sketch a diagram or initiate a web search. Yet "visioning" amounts to nothing without focused, sustained effort. A colleague once teased: "It's easy for you to be a visionary—you don't count the cost!"

As we assess the health and holiness of our discontent, we may sense God's call to act. Crazy ideas pop into our minds. Exciting possibilities fill our hearts. Increasingly, we yearn to pursue our dreams. As Frederick Buechner wrote, "the place God calls you to is the place where your deep gladness and the world's deep hunger meet."[21]

This sense of call requires specificity and singularity. We can't take on every project that come to mind, nor can we invest ourselves in every person or place with need. Saying "no" to good things is necessary if we are to give a whole-hearted "yes" to what God wants as our "main thing." Confirming our sense of call is crucial. We must ascertain whether our ideas are human delusions or God-given visions.

To gain confirmation, prepare to take steps of faith. At its essence, faith is the courage to act upon what you believe is true. Only by acting on your perception can you discover whether you are heeding God's voice. Begin by leveraging your assets, especially your influence.

DAY 8

TEST YOUR CALL

If we act upon the Lord's leadings, we can usually discern God's calling.

Let's return to Nehemiah's story. Through intense prayer, the Jewish cupbearer to the Persian emperor discerned that his discontent was holy and healthy. The action plan in his head seemed a God-given "leading". His next step was to test his call with a leap of faith. Consider his prayer:

> "O Lord, let your ear be attentive to the prayer of your servant, and to the prayer of your servants who delight in revering your name. Give success to your servant today, and grant him mercy in the sight of this man!"
> Nehemiah 1:11

Here's what happened next:

> In the month of Nisan, in the twentieth year of King Artaxerxes, when wine was served him, I carried the wine and gave it to the king. Now, I had never been sad in his presence before. So the king said to me, "Why is your face sad, since you are not sick? This can only be sadness of the heart." Then I was very much afraid.
> Nehemiah 2:1-2

The "month of Nisan, in the twentieth year of King Artaxerxes" indicates that this encounter took place in March-April of 444 B.C. Providentially, 142 years after the Jews were taken into exile, a Jewish servant leveraged his proximity to the most powerful man on earth and fulfilled God's redemptive purposes.

It's not appropriate for a server to engage those being served in conversation unless the recipients initiate the conversation. While a student in Washington, DC, one of our daughters worked at an upscale tavern. She was warned not to make comments or inquiries, especially when waiting upon celebrities or politicians.

Even if troubled, a professional server shouldn't share his or her burdens with clients. This emotional firewall was critical for a servant serving an emperor. Yet after much prayer, Nehemiah sensed the Spirit leading him to cross this boundary. As he poured and taste tested the king's wine, Nehemiah showed himself to be downcast. The king noticed and inquired, "Why is your face sad, since you are not sick? This can only be sadness of the heart."

Nehemiah wasn't manipulative, for his grief was authentic. But choosing to be honest was a daring move. It could backfire terribly. No wonder he was "very much afraid."

RELEASE AND RESOURCES

Artaxerxes' empathetic response was a huge relief. The king's compassion was a sign that Nehemiah's yearning was a call from God. Soon we will read how Artaxerxes released the cupbearer of his obligation. The king's willingness to be inconvenienced was a sign that God was at work. He became a generous partner. The resources needed to rebuild Jerusalem's walls became available because Nehemiah boldly leveraged his relational network.

Do you have responsibilities that might prevent you from embracing God's call? If volunteer commitments consume your time, God might confirm your call by providing substitutes for your other commitments. Seek confirmation by exploring whether others will release you from obligation, even at cost to them.

TESTING BY SHARING

The first way to test your call is to share your discontent in a careful, prayerful manner. It is ok—even commendable—to share your unhappiness when it's healthy and grounded in God! Start with your greatest asset, your network of relationships. While few of us work in proximity to a king or a president, we are connected to hundreds of people. Many of us are entrusted with dozens of personal relationships and a multitude of email "contacts" and social media "friends".

Your relational network may include people who share your holy discontent. Some will be eager to hear that you are ready to act. Others will be awakened from emotional slumber when you cast your vision. *Their enthusiasm will confirm that the call is from God.*

Leveraging relational networks often yields partnerships. Partners don't always participate on a personal level, yet they can still contribute to the cause. There will be people eager to contribute money to the cause for which you are passionate. Partners can also supply the names of other potential participants.

Ask the Spirit to give you leadings as to whom you should express your concern and how you should express it. Plead with God to guide you as you assess their response. Their support might be the key to confirming your plans.

The easiest method would be to broadcast your concern on social media, though a scattershot approach would likely yield a disappointing response. In the formative stages, it is better to select individuals with whom you can share your passion over coffee or lunch. Enhance your presentation with a single-page write-up, an attractive brochure, a series of photos, or a compelling video. Once a group of participants has coalesced, then it will be time to "go public" with announcements, social media, information meetings, or newspaper coverage.

Our sense of holy discontent with the institutional church prompted Lynn and me to plant Church in the Wild. We envisioned a highly relational and radically missional congregation.[22] To avoid self-delusion, we asked God to show us how to share our vision---and with whom. We met personally with several friends who were interested in the missional church movement. The response wasn't overwhelming, yet one friend offered her leadership experience and financial support. Two subsequent informational meetings were attended by several dozen people, most of whom signed up to participate.

Church in the Wild has grown slower than I expected. Our emphasis on opening our homes to neighbors can be intimidating to those accustomed to "going to church."[23] Nonetheless, we've been heartened by signs that God continues to confirm our vision. At one point, nearly everyone serving on our music team had been invited by an elderly participant who struck up conversation with fellow shoppers or workmen repairing her house. Social media posts highlighting our service projects brought other partners. In recent years, a missional outreach at a brewery (Bible on Tap) has engaged dozens of men without a spiritual family, ultimately bringing many of them and their loved ones into Church in the Wild's worship life.

If we sincerely seek to embody God's mission, the Almighty will be ready and able to provide what we need. As the Lord declared: "Indeed, every animal of the forest is mine, even the cattle on a thousand hills" (Psalm 50:10, ISV). Receiving provision also provides confirmation that the vision is from God.

PONDER POTENTIAL PARTNERS:

Names Prompted by the Spirit	Participants and/or Partner?	How to Share Vision?
1)		
2)		
3)		
4)		
5)		
6)		
7)		

Who might have interest in participating or partnering in your hope-building endeavor? Open your smart phone's Contacts app. Ask the Spirit to leading you as you scroll through the names. Pray over your potential partners using this chart:

DAY 9

MAKE THE ASK

Hope-building faith invites others into God's work. After King Artaxerxes took notice of the prophet's sadness, Nehemiah trusted God and opened his mouth:

> Then I was very much afraid. I said to the king, "May the king live forever! Why should my face not be sad, when the city, the place of my ancestors' graves, lies waste, and its gates have been destroyed by fire?" Then the king said to me, "What do you request?" So I prayed to the God of heaven. Then I said to the king, "If it pleases the king, and if your servant has found favor with you, I ask that you send me to Judah, to the city of my ancestors' graves, so that I may rebuild it."
>
> Nehemiah 2:2b-5

In recent decades, countless safety measures have made air travel uneventful. Many passengers hardly notice the takeoff; they continue to read or watch videos, oblivious to the fact that they are leaving the ground.

Not me! Though I trust the statistics claiming that air travel is the safest mode of transportation, when those engines rev up, I offer a silent prayer. A plane in the air can land safely after losing one or more engines. The emergency water-landing of U.S. Airways Flight 1549 (the "Miracle on the Hudson") was feasible because the airliner had reached an elevation of 2818 feet when it struck the geese that disabled its engines. But a friend who is a pilot once explained that if an engine is lost during takeoff, there isn't time to react. Once the pilot kicks in the throttle, there is no turning back.

THROTTLE UP

Nehemiah was "very much afraid," for he was about to go full throttle. When the king inquired about his sad face, he could have aborted the mission by making up an excuse for his demeanor. Putting his complete trust in God, Nehemiah made the ask. There was no turning back. After declaring his loyalty, Nehemiah reminded the Persian emperor of the sad state of his ancestral homeland: Why should my face not be sad, when the city, the place of my ancestors' graves, lies waste, and its gates have been destroyed by fire?" (Neh. 2:3).

What a stunning moment for Persia's royal court: a servant speaking out on geopolitical issues. A member of a subjugated minority complaining about mistreatment! Artaxerxes could have taken offense, for Jerusalem was under his authority. He could have penalized his servant but did quite the opposite. God's providential favor was fully evident when the king asked, "What is it you want?" (2:4b).

This dialogue is reminiscent of Esther's boldness when she spoke truth to power. A generation earlier, that beautiful young woman had hidden her Jewishness when chosen to be the bride of Xerxes, Artaxerxes' father. But when the king's high official conspired to kill all the Jews, Esther leveraged her power to save her people. As her adoptive father Mordecai declared, "Who knows, perhaps you have come to your royal position for such a time as this" (Esther 4:14b, CSB).

God had positioned Nehemiah in King Artaxerxes' court "for such a time as this". When the king asked him what he wanted, Nehemiah cast his hope-building vision: "If it pleases the king, and if your servant has found favor with you, I ask that you send me to Judah, to the city of my ancestors' graves, so that I may rebuild it" (2:5).

What an ask! Nehemiah not only requested that Artaxerxes remedy the distress in Jerusalem, he also asked the king to give up his trusted attendant. This request could be disruptive. After pioneering Jews resettled their homeland, the Persian kings allowed non-Jewish strongmen to dominate the region. Nehemiah's ask might destabilize the Persian empire. Allowing the Jews to fortify their capital could lead to a resurgent Jewish state.

LEVERAGE YOUR ASSETS

God's call puts each of us on our own faith-based "runway". When holy discontent yields God-given vision, the Spirit compels us to leverage our assets. We were entrusted with relationships and influence, so that "for such a time as this", we can make hope-building asks.

Making such requests can be uncomfortable. The response may be "no, thanks" or "no way." Saying "yes" may be cost donors money, time, and attention. More money can be earned. People's reservoir of time is always shrinking.

Nonetheless, if you believe that your hope-building vision is from God, don't hesitate to ask. *Those you ask are likely to grow spiritually if they choose to participate.* Scripture promises that the Lord will provide for their needs, for "God is able to make every grace overflow to you, so that in every way, always having everything you need, you may excel in every good work" (2 Corinthians 9:8, CSB).

Lynn and I are well-acquainted with making asks. Initially, asking for financial donations was daunting. But then we discovered the amazing relationship between "fund-raising" and "faith-raising". When helping Christ-followers trust in God's provision, generosity flourishes, especially when there are compelling opportunities to bless others.

Previously, you read of how Neighbor Up Brevard's leaders wrestled with the seemingly insurmountable goal of building the DOCK (Dorcas Outreach Center for Children). Around that time, the Chief Executive Officer of Melbourne's largest high-tech corporation and his wife began to participate in our church. As Lynn and I were praying for resources to build the DOCK, they invited us to travel with them to see an Orlando Magic basketball game.

Grateful for the opportunity to connect with these community leaders, we prayed for guidance and asked the Lord to open their hearts. Ten minutes into the trip, this CEO asked Lynn to tell him about her work in Booker T. Washington, Melbourne's most troubled neighborhood. I prayed silently as she shared compellingly. Five minutes later, Lynn ended with, "We'd love to have whatever help you can give us." He listened well. We enjoyed the game. It seemed likely that they would make a donation.

The following week, the CEO invited Lynn and Sister Irene to make a presentation to the corporation's foundation committee. Lynn assembled a team: Sister Irene and a few Neighbor Up board members. Though marginal in the world's eyes, Irene spoke with Spirit-anointed authority as she cast the DOCK vision. The professional training of her Neighbor Up partners was also self-evident. They made an awesome team. Even though Neighbor Up Brevard was a Christian organization, this high-tech corporation offered a $150,000 matching grant to build the DOCK. This commitment not only covered one third of the construction cost, it raised the non-profit organization's credibility among other funding sources. After God honored that big ask with this amazing response, the DOCK's fundraising was easy.

It can be more difficult to ask people to give their time, especially if you're inviting them to minister to needy people with messy lives. As you cast the God-given vision, some people will "make time". Of course, time isn't "made;" it's just that your hope-building vision elevates new priorities. Less important commitments fade as more meaningful endeavors are embraced.

QUESTIONS TO PONDER:

1. What was Nehemiah's greatest asset?
2. What did saying "yes" to Nehemiah cost the King of Persia?
3. How might Nehemiah's example change the way you make "asks"?

DAY 10

MAXIMIZE THE ASK

Be prepared to take "yes" for an answer.

> The king said to me (the queen also was sitting beside him), "How long will you be gone, and when will you return?" So it pleased the king to send me, and I set him a date. Then I said to the king, "If it pleases the king, let letters be given me to the governors of the province Beyond the River, that they may grant me passage until I arrive in Judah; and a letter to Asaph, the keeper of the king's forest, directing him to give me timber to make beams for the gates of the temple fortress, and for the wall of the city, and for the house that I shall occupy." And the king granted me what I asked, for the gracious hand of my God was upon me.
> Nehemiah 2:6-8

In the presence of the queen, the cupbearer asked the king to release him from his duties. Nehemiah was thrilled to hear the favorable response: "How long will you be gone, and when will you return?" (Neh. 2:6a). Not "how long *would* you be gone?" but "how long *will* you be gone?" With great joy Nehemiah testified that "it pleased the king to send me" (6b). What an amazing confirmation of God's call. As Proverbs 21:1 declares: The king's heart is a stream of water in the hand of the Lord; he turns it wherever he will."

The king did ask when Nehemiah would return, for his absence would be costly. Grateful for Artaxerxes' graciousness, Nehemiah "set a time."

It would be tempting to quit while ahead, excusing oneself once the king expressed his support. Not Nehemiah. In his prayer-preparation, the Spirit prompted him to maximize the ask. Permission to leave wouldn't be sufficient for the mission to succeed. Travel was precarious. Local authorities might refuse passage or extort bribes. Letters from the emperor "to the governors of Trans-Euphrates" would be invaluable.

Furthermore, Nehemiah knew that Jerusalem's restoration would require building materials, so he asked for a letter "to Asaph, the keeper of the king's forest, directing him to give me timber..." (2:8a). After Artaxerxes granted these requests, Nehemiah praised "the gracious hand of my God" (2:8b).

ASSESSING ASSETS

When holy discontent forges our hope-building vision, our first step is to assess what we can contribute. We each have money, possessions, time, skills, expertise, training, and life experiences that we can place in God's hands.

While our assets may seem modest, even five loaves and two fish given to Jesus fed a massive crowd (Luke 9:10-17). Trusting that God will provide, look afresh at your calendar and budget. Ask God to open your eyes to resources that can be rechanneled to advance God's reign: money wasted in frivolous spending, homes rarely opened for hospitality, and time spent on screens. Too often we allow expertise to fade and skills to atrophy. Assess what you can contribute before you ask others to invest themselves.

INCREMENTAL ASKS

It's often best to begin with modest requests. Invite people to serve for a set length of time and on a defined basis. Those you approach may not yet share your sense of holy discontent, have your same passion, or match your willingness to sacrifice. Their inclination may be to help you rather than your cause. But if they hear your story, if they allow you to cast your vision, and if they see the need themselves, the Lord can infect them with a yearning to invest themselves.

As they see what you see and feel what you feel, ask more of them. You are not asking for yourself. You are speaking for God! The Lord has shown you the urgency of building hope. Sometimes the answer will be "no". Hear that "no" as "not yet". People embrace commitment at varying paces. God will be working to rearrange their commitments to reflect divine priorities.

Among the most difficult "asks" are recruiting teachers for children. Many people are apprehensive about committing hours to prepare and teach on a weekly basis. Children's ministry directors learn to make a series of small, incremental asks. Every summer, we saw new faces in our Vacation Bible School t-shirts. With attentive support and close supervision, these adults often had a positive experience. Their exposure to children cultivated a yearning to make positive impact on future generations. Increasingly they shared their leader's vision—that the next generation know God and embody God's reign. Many sustained ongoing commitments.

Whether on behalf of an AIDS awareness walkathon or an Alzheimer's research golf tournament, Lynn's grandfather, Rev. Dr. Wright Spears, was famous for his passionate and persuasive use of the phone—well into his 90s. One friend declared that "every time Wright called me, I knew I was about to sign up for something I hadn't known that I wanted to do".

It's easy to procrastinate. Inviting others to serve can be awkward and exhausting. It might stretch our friendships. *Yet holy discontent requires making the ask.*

Making asks send us to our knees in prayer, because God promises to pour out His favor when we ask for help. We will discover what Jesus meant by ""Ask, and it will be given to you. Seek, and you will find. Knock, and the door will be opened to you (Matthew 7:7).

And if "no" or "not yet" is the answer, our trust in God can be evident in our gracious response.

QUESTIONS TO PONDER:

1. What kinds of "asks" are necessary as you pursue God's call upon you? What would an incremental approach look like in your context?
2. Think of a time you were asked to give time or money to a cause, and you were motivated to give generously. What made that "ask" effective?

DAY 11

SHADOW SIDE OF GOD'S FAVOR

When God says "yes," life can get complicated. As Nehemiah recalled:

And the king granted me what I asked, for the gracious hand of my God was upon me.

Then I came to the governors of the province Beyond the River, and gave them the king's letters. Now the king had sent officers of the army and cavalry with me. When Sanballat the Horonite and Tobiah the Ammonite official heard this, it displeased them greatly that someone had come to seek the welfare of the people of Israel.

Nehemiah 2:8b-10

God's response to Nehemiah's prayers was truly amazing: "the king granted me what I asked, for the gracious hand of my God was upon me" (Neh. 2:8b). Not only did Artaxerxes permit the royal cupbearer to leave his post, not only did the king provide Nehemiah with safe-conduct letters, he also "sent officers of the army and cavalry" (2:9b). In the ancient world, travel was perilous. The king's military escort greatly increased the likelihood of safe travel. God's provident hand had recruited a pagan emperor to rebuild the Jewish capital!

God doesn't always respond to our Kingdom-advancing prayers with such dramatic outpourings. We might correctly discern God's call and act upon the Spirit's leadings, yet the provision seems modest. It's possible to have a genuine call from God yet also struggle with disappointing outcomes. Paul reminded Timothy to "be ready in season and out of season" (2 Timothy 4:2a, CSB). Whatever the fruit of our labor, our satisfaction comes from pleasing God with our obedience and honoring God in our growth.

Sometimes God will magnify the impact of our efforts in ways that we couldn't have imagined. Partners step forward to participate. Free publicity boosts our efforts. Financial resources emerge from nowhere. "Persons of peace" welcome us into their relational network, opening doors to new opportunities (Luke 10:5-6, CSB). We won't know how God will provide until we act.

GOOD NEWS NOT ALWAYS WELCOME

Even when God's favor shines brightly on our hope-building, we might face a shadowy side to God's outpouring of resources. The good news that the Persians sponsored Nehemiah's restoration of Jerusalem was received as bad news to powerful people who benefitted from the city's vulnerability. Verse 10 foreshadows conflict on the horizon: "When Sanballat the Horonite and Tobiah the Ammonite official heard this, it displeased them greatly that someone had come to seek the welfare of the people of Israel."

Who were these guys? Sanballat led the Samaritan army (4:2). The Samaritans emerged after the Assyrian Empire conquered the ten northern tribes of Israel three hundred years earlier. After many Israelites were taken into exile, Assyrian invaders seized their property. Canaanites whose ancestors were expelled by Joshua returned to their ancestral home. Over time, many Jews who remained intermarried with the Assyrians and Canaanites. These racially and religiously mixed people were known as the Samaritans, adversaries to the Judeans and Galileans who remained ethnically and religious Jewish.

One hundred and thirty-six years after the Assyrian invasion of the Jews in the north, the Babylonians conquered the Jewish remnant in the south: Judea and its capital Jerusalem. Most Judeans were exiled to Babylon. Opportunistic enemies—Samaritans, Ammonites (Jordanians), and Arabians—moved into the vacated territory. Since Jews from the north didn't return, these Gentile settlers in the south didn't expect to deal with the Judean Jews again. They couldn't envision a pathway for exiled Jews to return, rebuild their cities, and restore their worship. Yet in time, the Persians conquered the Babylonians. Who could have imagined that pagan Persian kings would send Jews to resettle their homeland and rebuild their Temple, sponsoring this restoration with safe-conduct passes, troops, and cavalry?

Allied with Sanballat against the returning Jews was Tobiah, the leader of the Ammonites (Jordanians), as well as Geshem, the leader of the Arabs (See Nehemiah 2:19). The prospect that a rebuilt Jerusalem and restored Judea united them in opposition.

VERY MUCH DISTURBED

The undeniable reality is that the good news of God's redemptive and restorative work is often received as bad news to people who have benefitted from the *status quo*. When African Americans won victories in their struggle for civil rights, racists in the white majority were "very much disturbed". When neighbors unite to fight crime and revitalize their neighborhood, it's to be expected that drug dealers will be "very much disturbed". When alcoholics embrace sobriety, drinking buddies can be "very much disturbed". *Building hope can bring controversy.*

Community leaders can be "very much disturbed" by hope-building if they have a narcissistic need to control the changes in their neighborhood. When an online article in the newspaper celebrated Neighbor Up Brevard's replacement of drug-ridden, slum housing with safe, affordable apartments, a community leader trashed it with online comments. Though Neighbor Up had valued partnership with resident leaders, several others found fault with the ministry's success. When the DOCK's after school program attracted scores of teenagers seeking support in making positive choices, Neighbor Up Brevard made plans to build a Teen Center. Incredibly, a neighbor complained at a rezoning hearing that a building designed to keep teenagers off the street would create problems for the community. Happily, city officials heeded the teenagers who explained how growing up in the DOCK had stabilized their lives.

Even when a congregation takes steps to restore its health and renew its mission to its surrounding community, some of its members may be "very much disturbed". You would think that revitalizing a dying congregation would thrill everyone, yet those devoted to outdated traditions and ineffective programs can be "very much disturbed" by Spirit-led renewal.

Doing God's work may produce enemies who oppose what God wants you to do. On Day 22 we'll explore ways in which evil may oppose those who seek to build hope. Learning how Nehemiah outmaneuvered and overcame his enemies will provide invaluable insights. We'll also draw lessons from the New Testament. *Our greatest victories over evil occur as God uses us to make peace with enemies.* Christ-followers "do not think of anyone from a human point of view" for God "has given us the message of reconciliation" (2 Corinthians 5:16, 18, ISV). After a woman referred to Southerners as "irreconcilable enemies" who should be "destroyed," President Lincoln reportedly declared, "Madam, do I not destroy my enemies when I make them my friends?"[24]

A strong sense of holy discontent provides the passion that hope-builders need to overcome personal inertia. Organizing a hope-building effort requires tangible leadership skills. The next stages of Nehemiah's journey will teach us how to inspire others to pour themselves into our sacred work. There will be much wisdom to glean as we seek to enhance our capability.

QUESTIONS TO PONDER:

1. As you envision the minimal resources and necessary circumstances needed for your hope-building dream to become reality, what would be a sign of a beyond-your-expectations "favor"?

2. How might God-given effectiveness bring opposition to your work?

3. Do you remember a work or ministry-team conflict ending in repentance, confession, and reconciliation? If so, what were the key events that initiated a positive resolution?

DAY 12

QUIET DUE DILIGENCE

Hope-builders must do their "homework". As Nehemiah recalled:

So I came to Jerusalem and was there for three days. Then I got up during the night, I and a few men with me; I told no one what my God had put into my heart to do for Jerusalem. The only animal I took was the animal I rode. I went out by night by the Valley Gate past the Dragon's Spring and to the Dung Gate, and I inspected the walls of Jerusalem that had been broken down and its gates that had been destroyed by fire. Then I went on to the Fountain Gate and to the King's Pool; but there was no place for the animal I was riding to continue. So I went up by way of the valley by night and inspected the wall. Then I turned back and entered by the Valley Gate, and so returned. The officials did not know where I had gone or what I was doing; I had not yet told the Jews, the priests, the nobles, the officials, and the rest that were to do the work.   Nehemiah 2:11-16

Even after key supporters pledge their presence and their treasure, we might not be completely prepared for our God-given endeavor. Before going public, it would be prudent to invest more time in understanding the challenge and developing our strategy. Avoiding poor decisions and wasted efforts makes it more likely that our work will be successful and sustainable.

Allied Supreme Commander General Dwight Eisenhower dedicated years to planning D-Day, the key battle in the effort to liberate Europe from Nazi rule. Despite this meticulous preparation, on June 6, 1941, the battle did not go as planned. On the eve of the attack, Allied battleships were supposed to pummel the French coastline with artillery fire to create large craters so that ground troops wading ashore could take cover. Tragically, most of the big guns missed their targets. When the first wave of troops stormed the beach, few craters were available. Two-thirds of the first company were killed on the beach. Nonetheless, other aspects of the planning sustained the attack, and Eisenhower was prepared to adapt. When the sun set on D-Day, the Allied foothold in France was secure.

In reflecting on his experience as a leader, Eisenhower said that "in preparing for battle, I have always found that plans are worthless, but planning is everything"[25]

After launching into hope-building, you will encounter endless surprises. Events will not unfold as you expect. Some surprises will be positive, others will be setbacks. Who could have imagined the impact of the COVID-19 pandemic? Probably, your initial plans will be inadequate. Yet it's crucial to learn all that you can and plan as best as you can.

TACTICAL SILENCE

Nehemiah likely learned much about Jerusalem while still in Persia. He probably sought a detailed description from his brother Hanani and anyone else who knew the city's layout. Perhaps he drew up preliminary maps of the city walls and gates. Upon arrival, a foolish leader might have announced his plans with fanfare. After all, King Artaxerxes had endorsed his project. Nonetheless. Nehemiah didn't say anything for three days as he rested from the long trip.

Nehemiah demonstrated the wisdom of tactical silence. He wanted to learn in secret before he spoke in public. Having "told no one what God had put into my heart to do for Jerusalem," Nehemiah and a few men "got up during the night". He kept a low profile, taking no animal other than the one on which he road (Neh. 2:12). In verse 16 he recalled that "the officials did not know where I had gone or what I was doing; I had not yet told the Jews, the priests, the nobles, the officials, and the rest that were to do the work."

Nehemiah's silence was wise. Once he spoke publicly, opponents such as Sanballat and Tobiah would scramble to sabotage his efforts. If Nehemiah hesitated after speaking, the project might never get off the ground.

Even if your hope-building effort seems unlikely to stir up opponents, it's wise to pursue due diligence before you launch into the effort. Become an expert. Develop your battle plan.

PURPOSE-DRIVEN PREPARATION

Several decades ago, I became the senior pastor of a large congregation that wasn't effective in cultivating spiritual growth. Hundreds of people were drawn to meaningful worship services, but only a fraction of the congregation participated in classes, small groups, or ministry teams. As holy discontent gripped my heart, I read dozens of books on congregational effectiveness. Eventually I discerned that God was calling our leaders to transform our complacent congregation into a "purpose-driven" church.

My associate pastor and I presented our vision for retooling our ministry programs to our church's elders. Remarkably, our vision received enthusiastic support. Yet still we didn't "go public" to the congregation. First, we invested many hours into personal preparation, anticipating every possible issue and obstacle. Our staff and elders held extra meetings and developed a strategic timeline. These plans would change. Yet taking the time to prepare before we embarked was exceedingly wise. Even though nearly everyone wanted the church to have greater impact, almost every change required "killing a sacred cow," stirring opposition.

The description of Nehemiah's night ride graphically illustrates the overwhelming challenge. If he had underestimated the work, no longer could he ignore the immense challenge of rebuilding massive stone walls, for they were "broken down…the gates had been "destroyed by fire" (2:13). Near the Fountain Gate the piles of rubble didn't allow his horse room to walk. Yet God-given hope swelled Nehemiah's heart as he made mental notes.

UNDERSTANDING TO BE UNDERSTOOD

Your next step in hope-building will be to speak words that inspire others. One of Stephen Covey's "seven habits of highly effective people" is "seek first to understand…then be understood".[26] *Due diligence prior to casting vision is crucial if you want to be a credible communicator with those you seek to persuade.* You will gain this knowledge by reading, listening, and immersing yourself in the project's details. If you seek to renew a church or restore a neighborhood, interview "long-timers" who can give you a grasp of its history. Perhaps you would benefit from training, a mentor, or a personal coach.

Tactical silence and due diligence require a healthy measure of humility. Having holy discontent about a situation doesn't mean that you are prepared to fix it. Quick "yesses" to your asks shouldn't delude you into assuming that hope-building is a breeze. Jim Collins wrote, "You absolutely cannot make a series of good decisions without first confronting the brutal facts."[27]

You face the facts of what is wrong and what will be required by taking your own version of Nehemiah's night ride. This reality-therapy might send you to your knees. With humility, ask God to do what you cannot do on your own. As James the brother of Jesus reminded the church: "God opposes the proud, but gives grace to the humble" (James 4:6b).

Pausing to understand the challenges before you embark can be disconcerting. Lingering on the precipice tempts you to give up before you start. Nonetheless, you'll do well to develop an action plan before taking the plunge.

QUESTIONS TO PONDER:

1. Why was it crucial for Nehemiah to take his "night ride" before he spoke publicly?
2. Have you spent time in seeking to understand the problems you want to remedy? If not, what books or article might you read? What people might you interview?
3. Have you written out goals and expectations? A tentative timeline? A tentative budget (if applicable)?
4. Might it be prudent to keep your plans hidden from some people?

INSPIRE OTHERS TO ACTION

Few experiences are more meaningful than uniting people in hope. With deep satisfaction, Nehemiah remembered the day that God used his words to rally a city:

> Then I said to them, "You see the trouble we are in, how Jerusalem lies in ruins with its gates burned. Come, let us rebuild the wall of Jerusalem, so that we may no longer suffer disgrace." I told them that the hand of my God had been gracious upon me, and also the words that the king had spoken to me. Then they said, "Let us start building!" So they committed themselves to the common good. But when Sanballat the Horonite and Tobiah the Ammonite official, and Geshem the Arab heard of it, they mocked and ridiculed us, saying, "What is this that you are doing? Are you rebelling against the king?" Then I replied to them, "The God of heaven is the one who will give us success, and we his servants are going to start building; but you have no share or claim or historic right in Jerusalem."
>
> Nehemiah 2:17-20

Holy discontent burns within you. The Lord has channeled your unhappiness into a yearning for positive action. You believe that you see the way forward. You've tested your emerging vision by sharing it with potential participants and partners. Perhaps you have sensed God's hand at work as you've built a team for hope-building adventure.

Whether this narrative describes your recent journey, or whether you are still pondering how holy discontent can become hope-building, today's Nehemiah briefing provides a thrilling glimpse of how God-given vision becomes reality. After his night ride fulfilled his due diligence, Nehemiah broke his silence, seeking to inspire everyone who could hear. These included "the priests, the nobles, the officials, and the rest who were to do the work," everyone available to rebuild the wall (Neh. 2:16). If Nehemiah were alive today, he would surely post his wall-building plans on social media.

His speech was vision casting par *excellence*. Nehemiah began by naming brutal facts, "You see the trouble we are in, how Jerusalem lies in ruins with its gates burned" (2:17a). You would think that the horrible status quo would be obvious to everyone, but people often become accustomed to their negative situation. Courageously naming brutal facts fosters the likelihood that complacent people will rediscover long-repressed discontent.

BRUTAL FACTS

Naming the brutal facts is crucial for church leaders who seek to cultivate positive change. Eighty percent of the churches in America are in decline or on a plateau[28] (prior to the disruptive impact of the COVID pandemic). Most experts predict that the decline of American church participation will accelerate, as it has in Europe. Without fully facing the reality that North America is rapidly becoming a post-Christian mission field, church members delude themselves in assuming that simply getting a younger pastor or changing the worship style will restore a congregation's vitality.

But just naming brutal facts doesn't inspire people. Without infusing hope, confronting complacency yields despair. Nehemiah didn't linger on the bad news that "Jerusalem lies in ruins." He pivoted, challenging them to join him in restoring the security and the prominence of their city: "Come, let us rebuild the wall of Jerusalem, so that we may no longer suffer disgrace" (2:17b).

VISION CASTING

"Vision casting" is often perceived as a skill possessed by gifted, charismatic leaders. Actually, many people are capable of casting vision. It's remarkably simple. First, name the brutal facts. Second, announce your preferred outcome—describing its appearance and the benefits it will bring for the community. Then declare your personal commitment to this hopeful future. Finally, share the news of how God has already begun to provide partners and resources. Nehemiah recalled he "told them that the hand of my God had been gracious upon me, and also the words that the king had spoken to me." (2:18a). We can imagine the Persian cupbearer repeatedly describing how he had shared his holy discontent with Artaxerxes. Likely he relished telling how the king not only released him from service, but also provided safe passage and building materials.

The people's response was immediate and enthusiastic: "'Let us start building...so they committed themselves to the common good" (2:18b). Of course, there would be logistics to coordinate and problems to solve. But suddenly everything had changed. Jerusalem overflowed with hope. The collective energies of its population were unleashed. Previously complacent people will make remarkable sacrifices when inspired by leaders who are "all in".

I have vivid memories of vision casting for church building campaigns. In striving to persuade church members to give sacrificially ("above and beyond" the operating budget), the key was to recognize that "fund-raising" requires "faith-raising." The greatest obstacle to a financial campaign isn't a shortage of money but a "shortage mentality" in the minds of God's people. On an individual level, people with a "shortage mentality" fear that "I won't have enough for myself if I give away more." Regarding their congregation, those with "shortage mentality" perceive that "we can't do this…we can barely cover our regular expenses."

To overcoming such a mindset, cultivate an "abundance mentality". After highlighting the need and demonstrating your own commitment, recall how God has provided in the past. Remind your audience that God's Word promises provision to His people whenever they demonstrate their trust:

> Honor the Lord with your possessions
> and with the first produce of your entire harvest;
> then your barns will be completely filled,
> and your vats will overflow with new wine.   Proverbs 3:9-10, CSB

My first seminal experience as a vision casting pastor was leading a capital campaign of a small congregation comprised of modest income households. Though its giving potential seemed low, the congregation saw the need and recognized my commitment. Despite their lack of wealth, by trusting in God's provision, they eagerly increased their giving. This remarkable generosity probably required several of them to drive old cars longer, eat out less often, and take fewer vacations. Their sacrifices enabled a new sanctuary to be built in an old neighborhood, a remarkable sign of faith-raising.

Many years later, as the pastor of a more affluent congregation, I led a capital campaign with a much larger financial goal. While the task might have seemed easier, the obstacles were greater. Just because people have high incomes doesn't mean that they perceive themselves having the ability for greater generosity. The sad truth is that with affluence often comes an insatiable appetite for expensive homes, luxury cars, and exotic vacations. High-income people often live above their means. To make matters worse, after we announced our plan to raise millions of dollars, the east coast of Florida was slammed by two major hurricanes in three weeks. Florida wind insurance policies have a deductible of at least two percent of each home's appraised value. Almost every household had to scrounge $5,000 to $15,000 to cover the repair deductible.

It didn't seem a good time to ask for extra giving commitments. But with thorough vision casting, our congregation rallied to reach the goal. We demonstrated the need and explained the construction plans. Because of rumors that we might move to another congregation, Lynn and I assured the church of our commitment to remain in the community. We also shared our decision to take out a loan equivalent to a tenth of the increase in our home value, which enabled us to double our contribution. This "all-in" leadership encouraged hundreds of households to wrestle with their own commitments. The campaign was called "Because We Believe!" Because we believed, we exceeded our goal.

ABUNDANCE MENTALITY

Vision casting isn't just to get things done. *We challenge people to trust God in tangible ways so they can discover how God will provide.* The Lord uses our vision casting to thwart the tendency for a "shortage mentality" to take hold among God's people. We cultivate an "abundance mentality," for "God is able to make every grace overflow to you, so that in every way, always having everything you need, you may excel in every good work." (2 Corinthians 9:8, CSB). Whether fundraising, recruiting volunteers, launching programs, or forming missional communities, faith-raising succeeds as God magnifies the influence of leaders who channel their holy discontent into hope-building vision, "For the eyes of the Lord range throughout the entire earth, to strengthen those whose heart is true to him" (2 Chronicles 16:9a).

God's favor doesn't obliterate our challenges. In a fallen world, hope's bright light often renders dark shadows. Sanballat, Tobiah, and Geshem comprised an unholy trinity to oppose Nehemiah's redemptive activity. Previously, we read that they were "very much disturbed" to hear of his arrival. After Nehemiah's public proclamation of hope, his opponents "ridiculed". They fired their first shot, accusing Nehemiah of disloyalty to Artaxerxes: "Are you rebelling against the king?" (2:19b).

Nehemiah's response was bold. Instead of squirming in fear and insisting on his loyalty to Artaxerxes, he declared his confidence in the Lord God Almighty, the King of creation: "The God of heaven in the one who will give us success, and we his servants are going to start building; but you have no share or claim or historic right in Jerusalem" (2:20). Nehemiah's hope-building would not flinch in the face of opposition to God's redemptive work.

The spirit of Sanballat, Tobiah, and Geshem stalks us, also. Just prior to launching the "Because We Believe" campaign, a "very much disturbed" woman mocked me for daring to believe that God would raise our faith and millions of dollars only six months after devastating hurricanes: "You will fall on your face," she hissed over the phone. While I have fallen on my face at other times, rarely have I felt stronger and steadier than the season of leading Because We Believe.

Not everyone is prepared to give inspirational speeches or is gifted in vision casting. *Yet each of us can stand with someone giving visionary leadership.* While every incarnation of hope-building needs at least one Nehemiah, God also uses quiet leaders who inspire others with quietly courageous actions. The "Nehemiahs" of the world would have little impact if not for faithful followers also transformed by holy discontent.

QUESTIONS TO PONDER:

1. Why is it crucial to "name brutal facts" prior to offering words of inspiration?
2. Why does vision casting require us to declare our own costly commitment?
3. What does it mean to say that spiritually grounded "fund-raising" requires "faith-raising"?

DAY 14

IN-FILL SUSTAINS OVERFLOW

Stay connected to your Source. Jesus said,

I am the vine, you are the branches. The one who abides in me while I abide in him produces much fruit, because apart from me you can do nothing. Unless a person abides in me, he is thrown away like a pruned branch and dries up. People gather such branches, throw them into a fire, and they are burned up.

"If you abide in me and my words abide in you, you can ask for anything you want, and you'll receive it. This is how my Father is glorified, when you produce a lot of fruit and so prove to be my disciples. Just as the Father has loved me, so I have loved you. So abide in my love. If you keep my commandments, you'll abide in my love, just as I have kept my Father's commandments and abide in his love. I've told you this, so that my joy may be in you, and that your joy may be complete.   John 15:5-11, ISV

After two weeks of discovering how God can channel holy discontent into positive action, let's pause to consider how God will sustain your efforts. Living on God's mission is not a weekend road trip. It is an enduring odyssey. When I was an exchange student at the United Theological College of the West Indies, my classmates often declared with exaggerated Jamaican accents: "De journey is LONG."

Your hope-building journey may seem long. You might be tripped up or tempted to give up. You will need the Lord's strength to keep on when exhausted and to pick yourself up after you fall.

I have a psychologist friend who urges listeners to care for themselves so they can sustain caregiving for others. He reminds his patients that when flight attendants review the emergency procedures, parents are told that if the oxygen masks drop from overhead, they should secure their own mask first before attempting to place masks on their children.

Finding strength for the journey is crucial to our success. Some of the wisdom we've gleaned from Nehemiah can be found in secular self-help guides or books on leadership. Yet Nehemiah's journey spotlights God's indispensable role in empowering God's people. Move in concert with God's leading. Act in confidence that God's power will magnify your efforts.

OUR DIVINE SOURCE

Two biblical metaphors highlight our infinite and eternal Source. Before handing over his Father's mission on earth, Jesus reminded his disciples that "I am the vine, you are the branches...apart from me you can do nothing" (John 15:5, ISV). Secular people can surely do good things. By "apart from me you can do nothing," Jesus meant that as cut branches wither, without him our efforts would lack divine power and eternal significance. As the psalmist wrote, "Unless the Lord builds the house, its builders labor uselessly" (127:1, ISV).

To bear authentic spiritual fruit, develop a rhythm of giving time and attention to Jesus as well as serving Jesus with good deeds. Martha complained to Jesus when her sister Mary sat at his feet instead of preparing the meal. In great love, Jesus corrected her: "Martha, Martha, you are worried and upset about many things, but one thing is necessary. Mary has made the right choice, and it will not be taken away from her" (Luke 10:41-42, CSB). Not only does the Lord challenge you to be a "Martha," doing his work, he also insists that you be a "Mary," at times giving him undivided attention. Disciples who feed upon God's Word and listen for the Spirit's leading are far more productive. As Jesus said, "The one who abides in me while I abide in him produces much fruit" (John 15:5b, ISV).

The second biblical image of God's sustenance is a water barrel. As Paul declared, "May God, the source of hope, fill you with joy and peace through your faith in him. Then you will overflow with hope by the power of the Holy Spirit." (Romans 15:13, GW). Normally the water in a barrel is depleted as the water is consumed, but if the barrel has been configured to capture the rainfall, will fill to overflowing.

It's easy to maintain a positive attitude when you see encouraging signs or hear upbeat reports. But when disappointments pile up or opposition mounts, your vision may fade and your energy run low, unless you trust in God to "fill you with joy and peace" (Romans 15:13a, GW). The key is the phrase "through your faith in him". Trusting God to do what He has promised opens spiritual conduits that deliver a steady stream of joy and peace. As we will hear Nehemiah testify when Jerusalem gathers to worship: "the joy of the LORD is your strength" (Nehemiah 8:10).

HOW TO RECEIVE

Your clearest expression of trust is obedience—to do what Jesus has commanded. Yet obedience is difficult if peace and joy fade. It seems a circular dilemma. To receive an infusion of God's hope and joy, you must trust in God. But what if you lack faith because you are discouraged?

The good news is that God doesn't abandon us when our faith flags. The Lord works relentlessly to free us from the shackles of discouragement. God has spoken through the written Word and the ever-present Spirit; he also encourages us with fellow disciples. If we embody habits that position us to receive, we'll be nourished and refreshed.

Read scripture each day, especially if you're discouraged. Read until you find what is helpful. When I suffered great anguish, I found great balm in the psalms of lament. These ancient expressions of distress give voice to your pain as you read them aloud. Their placement in the Bible underscores God's desire for us to name our disappointments, even our questions. Jesus called out the first words of Psalm 22, "My God, my God, why have you forsaken me?" His prayer helped Jesus endure the cross (Mark 15:34). Claiming ancient words of lament as my own was cathartic, helping me to grasp God's identification with my suffering. Eventually, green shoots of hope and joy sprung into my barren heart.

Continue the habits of fellowship. Even if you must drag yourself to worship or small group gatherings, take care of yourself by interacting with God's people. God sustains our good works by using Christian community to encourage us. As the preacher of Hebrews proclaimed, "…let us consider how to provoke one another to love and good deeds, not neglecting to meet together, as is the habit of some, but encouraging one another, and all the more as you see the Day approaching" (Hebrews 10:24-25a).

Staying connected in meaningful relationships provides huge benefits. According to the scriptures, our Lord created the church so we can "bear one another's burdens" (Galatians 6:2), "encourage one another and build up each other" (1 Thessalonians 5:11), "equip the saints for the work of ministry (Ephesians 4:12), "speaking the truth in love" to each other (Ephesians 4:15), as we "teach and admonish one another" (Colossians 3:16). Unfortunately, many churches pretend that sharing refreshments after worship qualifies as genuine fellowship. Whatever the size of your congregation, seek to develop authentic and attentive relationships with a realistic number of believers.

Continue in the habit of prayer. When your mind drifts, write your prayers in a journal. Ask the Holy Spirit to remind you of the many ways you have been blessed. Write them down. Read them out loud, for Paul wrote "…with thanksgiving, let your requests be made known to God" (Philippians 4:6). Try various postures for prayer. Sometimes I kneel to concentrate. Other times, I pray while on a long walk. Keep a list of the people and circumstances that occupy your prayer. When a concern has been answered, write it down. Keep a list and read over it.

Those who build hope know that persistent prayer is powerful. Paradoxically, prayer is the easiest habit to neglect. No wonder our efforts are often fruitless.

DEVOTED TO PRAYER

Western church leaders who hear of the remarkable growth of Christianity in Korea often ask church leaders, "What's your secret?" The frequent response from Korean church leaders is this: "We have many prayer meetings. Often, we gather very early on workdays simply to pray." Western Christians often reply, "Yes, I know that prayer is important, but really, what's the secret to your growth?" The Korean Christians reply, "That's it, prayer is the secret."

Eventually, it may dawn on us that only God can soften hardened hearts and open closed minds. Only the Holy Spirit can transform spiritual babies into mature Christ-followers. If we truly believe what we claim about God, faithfulness in prayer is the secret for sustaining vital, hope-building ministry.

I once had the privilege of spending five days with a partner congregation in southern India: Bethel Mission Church in Kolar Gold Fields, east of Bangalore. Pastor Frank Godberg and his gracious wife Gladys hosted me. Previously, Lynn and I had hosted Pastor Frank in our home. During the twenty years that I've known Pastor Frank, Bethel Mission Church has grown from 500 to 6,000 souls. Approximately 2,000 people worship at the main campus, the remainder at more than 40 satellite congregations led by pastors trained by Pastor Frank. Virtually everyone in Bethel Mission Church has converted to Christianity from Hinduism.

When I arrived, I was already aware of the centrality of prayer in the life of Bethel Mission Church. But imagine my surprise when my host politely explained that he would not join Gladys and me for meals because my visit coincided with his forty days of fasting and prayer. Each night Pastor Frank spent hours in prayer with several of the church's elders in a prayer room built on the rooftop. Mustering up the nerve, one night I asked if I could join them on the roof. It was my great privilege to pray with such spiritual warriors.

As we resume our reading of Nehemiah, we will see how he orchestrated teamwork and overcame opposition...because he first succeeded in private prayer.

QUESTIONS TO PONDER:

1. If Jesus will not abandon us, how is it possible for us not to abide in Christ?
2. How do we demonstrate our trust in the God of hope?
3. If you "overflow with hope," what will be your effect on those around you?
4. What reasons do Western Christians give for investing little time in prayer?
5. What is your biggest obstacle to a meaningful prayer life? What suggestions might help you break the impasse?

WEEK 3
Nehemiah 3:1-32

ORCHESTRATE TEAMWORK

No matter the depth of Nehemiah's holy discontent, the richness of his prayer life, and his prowess in raising resources, Jerusalem's rubble wouldn't become a wall without remarkable teamwork. The project was huge and time was short. The tasks were dirty, degrading, and dangerous. Rivalry, controversy, and sloth were ever-present hurdles. Fear of invasion brought constant distraction. Yet through this Spirit-led leader, God united people in shared sacrifice.

Because of Jesus, God's people no longer aspire to build walls. We strive to build relational bridges and restore communities. Yet the necessity to orchestrate teamwork is unchanging.

From Nehemiah, we'll see how teamwork builds social cohesion and discover how self-interest can benefit the community. Inasmuch as we make the greatest impact by empowering others, we'll explore how to cultivate servants' hearts and equip others to build hope.

DAY 15

BUILD HOPE TO BUILD COMMUNITY

The best part of a community project is how it builds community—an experience to be treasured.

Have you noticed that when teenagers prepare to go on a mission trip, a looming challenge is fundraising? Rather than sell overpriced stuff that few people need, our student ministry director developed a tradition of helping students enlist "shareholders" to buy "stock" in their endeavor. Each student was encouraged to send a personalized version of a sample letter to a list of adults within the congregation. The letter explained the goals of the mission trip and asked recipients to invest in the cause. When the students returned, the investors were invited to a "Shareholders' Banquet." After serving a scrumptious meal, the students reported on their trip—with hundreds of photos.

These Shareholders Banquets were prized by those who were emotionally invested in the trip (students, leaders, parents, and grandparents). Those attending learned a little about the slums of Haiti or the gritty streets of South Side, Chicago, but most photos featured "who did what" and "who suffered what prank." To outsiders, such inside jokes could wear thin. Yet those personally invested relished the evening. Remembering details authenticated their experience.

Chapter 3 of Nehemiah is a "Shareholders' Report" that dates back 2,400 years. These details were treasured by the generation who rebuilt Jerusalem's walls. The names and places have also been relished by faithful Jews throughout the centuries, an enduring reminder of the awesome impact of God's people when united in hope-building.

JERUSALEM'S SHAREHOLDER REPORT

We approach this text as outsiders. It's tempting to scan (or skip over) Nehemiah 3. Resist the temptation. For the remainder of Week 3, we'll focus on a few verses each day, gleaning biblical principles for organizing God's people for God's work. *Today, let's simply read and relish the historic details of this amazing undertaking.* Like watching a student mission trip PowerPoint presentation, the details underscore the authenticity. Trace Nehemiah's account of the gates' rebuilding using the diagram (page 77) and the model of the rebuilt city (page 78).[29]

The high priest Eliashib and his fellow priests were up and at it: They went to work on the Sheep Gate; they repaired it and hung its doors, continuing on as far as the Tower of the Hundred and the Tower of Hananel. The men of Jericho worked alongside them; and next to them, Zaccur son of Imri.

The Fish Gate was built by the Hassenaah brothers; they repaired it, hung its doors, and installed its bolts and bars. Meremoth son of Uriah, the son of Hakkoz, worked; next to him Meshullam son of Berekiah, the son of Meshezabel; next to him Zadok son of Baana; and next to him the Tekoites (except for their nobles, who wouldn't work with their master and refused to get their hands dirty with such work).

The Jeshanah Gate was rebuilt by Joiada son of Paseah and Meshullam son of Besodeiah; they repaired it, hung its doors, and installed its bolts and bars. Melatiah the Gibeonite, Jadon the Meronothite, and the men of Gibeon and Mizpah, which was under the rule of the governor from across the Euphrates, worked alongside them. Uzziel son of Harhaiah of the goldsmiths' guild worked next to him, and next to him Hananiah, one of the perfumers. They rebuilt the wall of Jerusalem as far as the Broad Wall.

The next section was worked on by Rephaiah son of Hur, mayor of a half-district of Jerusalem. Next to him Jedaiah son of Harumaph rebuilt the front of his house; Hattush son of Hashabneiah worked next to him.

Malkijah son of Harim and Hasshub son of Pahath-Moab rebuilt another section that included the Tower of Furnaces. Working next to him was Shallum son of Hallohesh, mayor of the other half-district of Jerusalem, along with his daughters.

The Valley Gate was rebuilt by Hanun and villagers of Zanoah; they repaired it, hung its doors, and installed its bolts and bars. They went on to repair 1,500 feet of the wall, as far as the Dung Gate.

The Dung Gate itself was rebuilt by Malkijah son of Recab, the mayor of the district of Beth Hakkerem; he repaired it, hung its doors, and installed its bolts and bars.

The Fountain Gate was rebuilt by Shallun son of Col-Hozeh, mayor of the Mizpah district; he repaired it, roofed it, hung its doors, and installed its bolts and bars. He also rebuilt the wall of the Pool of Siloam at the King's Garden as far as the steps that go down from the City of David.

After him came Nehemiah son of Azbuk, mayor of half the district of Beth Zur. He worked from just in front of the Tomb of David as far as the Pool and the House of Heroes.

Levites under Rehum son of Bani were next in line. Alongside them, Hashabiah, mayor of half the district of Keilah, represented his district in the rebuilding. Next to him their brothers continued the rebuilding under Binnui son of Henadad, mayor of the other half-district of Keilah.

The section from in front of the Ascent to the Armory as far as the Angle was rebuilt by Ezer son of Jeshua, the mayor of Mizpah.

From the Angle to the door of the house of Eliashib the high priest was done by Baruch son of Zabbai. Meremoth son of Uriah, the son of Hakkoz, took it from the door of Eliashib's house to the end of Eliashib's house. Priests from the neighborhood went on from there. Benjamin and Hasshub worked on the wall in front of their house, and Azariah son of Maaseiah, the son of Ananiah, did the work alongside his house.

The section from the house of Azariah to the Angle at the Corner was rebuilt by Binnui son of Henadad. Palal son of Uzai worked opposite the Angle and the tower that projects from the Upper Palace of the king near the Court of the Guard. Next to him Pedaiah son of Parosh and The Temple support staff who lived on the hill of Ophel worked up to the point opposite the Water Gate eastward and the projecting tower. The men of Tekoa did the section from the great projecting tower as far as the wall of Ophel.

Above the Horse Gate the priests worked, each priest repairing the wall in front of his own house. After them Zadok son of Immer rebuilt in front of his house and after him Shemaiah son of Shecaniah, the keeper of the East Gate; then Hananiah son of Shelemiah and Hanun, the sixth son of Zalaph; then Meshullam son of Berekiah rebuilt the wall in front of his storage shed.

Malkijah the goldsmith repaired the wall as far as the house of The Temple support staff and merchants, up to the Inspection Gate, and the Upper Room at the Corner. The goldsmiths and the merchants made the repairs between the Upper Room at the Corner and the Sheep Gate.   Nehemiah 3:1-32, MSG

Jerusalem's Wall in Nehemiah's Day

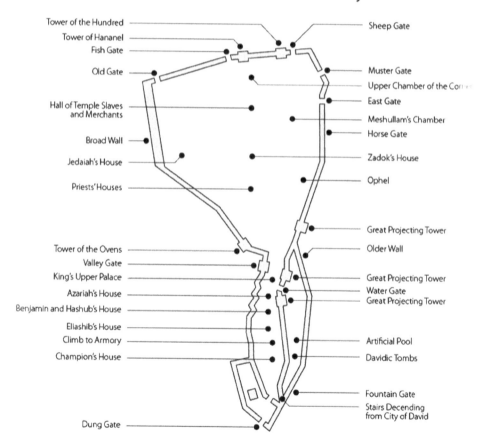

If you read the entirety of this ancient shareholders' celebration, you can better appreciate what God can accomplish whenever His people labor as one.

QUESTIONS TO PONDER:

1. What was interesting in the detailed account of the various groups and the specific locations of their work?
2. Did this overview provide you with any new principles for organizing work teams?
3. Does your hope-building team give sufficient attention to taking photos and celebrating how God brought you together?

DAY 16

RALLY SELF-INTERESTED INSIDERS

We humans were created to work in harmony. Our Creator designed us to be social beings who benefit from amazing productivity and remarkable efficiencies when we cooperate and collaborate. Sin compromises these positive outcomes. God's redemptive activity restores our capacity to work together for mutual blessing.

Providing human communities with wise leaders is a powerful expression of God's love. As we look close at Nehemiah 3, it's fascinating to observe how Nehemiah appealed to the self-interest of family units as he organized the wall building.

For example, shepherds used the Sheep Gate to bring their herds into Jerusalem near the Temple to be sacrificed. The Temple priests lived nearby, and so we are told that:

> The high priest Eliashib and his fellow priests were up and at it: They went to work on the Sheep Gate; they repaired it and hung its doors, continuing on as far as the Tower of the Hundred and the Tower of Hananel. Nehemiah 3:1, MSG

In the same way, Nehemiah leveraged each family's natural motivation to rebuild the walls bordering their homes in due haste and without flaw:

> Benjamin and Hasshub worked on the wall in front of their house, and Azariah son of Maaseiah, the son of Ananiah, did the work alongside his house. Nehemiah 3:23, MSG

We can envision the pride each household took in repairing the walls where they lived:

> Above the Horse Gate the priests worked, each priest repairing the wall in front of his own house. After them Zadok son of Immer rebuilt in front of his house and after him Shemaiah son of Shecaniah, the keeper of the East Gate; then Hananiah son of Shelemiah and Hanun, the sixth son of Zalaph; then Meshullam son of Berekiah rebuilt the wall in front of his storage shed.
>
> Nehemiah 3:28-30, MSG

The wisdom of appealing to self-interest seems obvious. In secular endeavors this principle is indisputable. Yet God's people can be squeamish in naming the reality that pursuing God's mission may involve appealing to healthy self-interest. We act as if community-blessing endeavors must be charitable to have legitimacy. On the contrary, the Christian community development movement insists that mutual self-interest can be superior to charity in fostering human betterment.

AVOID TOXIC CHARITY

When human need is urgent or life-threatening, God's people rightfully respond with charity. Yet often our charitable impulse becomes toxic. "Toxic charity" is generosity that dehumanizes recipients, robbing them of dignity and cultivating dependency. Toxic charity also robs well-resourced people the opportunity to enjoy mutually beneficial relationships with under-resourced people, neighbors who have inherent worth and valuable assets, despite their poverty.

Well-meaning leaders often do tasks that people can do for themselves. We do well to seek community development that harnesses self-interest. Mutually beneficial work partnerships are more enjoyable, yield better outcomes, and are easier to sustain.

One of the clearest voices in sounding the alarm about toxic charity belongs to Robert Lupton. Bob literally wrote the book.[30] His family relocated to inner city Atlanta in the 1980s and founded FCS Urban Ministries. Lynn became familiar with his work through the Christian Community Development Association's annual conferences. After we decided to relocate to the Booker T. Washington Neighborhood in Melbourne, we reached out to Bob. He graciously gave me an hour on the phone to draw upon his experience.

A HAND UP INSTEAD OF A HANDOUT

Because few young people in the Booker T. Washington have access to entry level jobs, I envisioned that our presence would provide opportunities to employ teenagers in building our fence and cutting grass. I hoped this experience would prepare them for their first real jobs. But what if one of these enterprising young men wanted to cut other people's yards? Should I loan him the equipment to make extra money? Not to loan the equipment seemed stingy, since I could afford to replace the equipment when it wore out.

I put the question to Bob. He didn't hesitate: "Charge them one or two dollars each time they use your equipment on other peoples' yards. Explain that you will need to replace the equipment sooner because of their use, and they should bear the extra cost." Otherwise, my generosity would be toxic.

Whenever we build hope, *let's remember that we are also in the people-development enterprise* (more on Week 5). Our initial impulse is to do much of the work and bear most of the cost because we aspire to be servant leaders like our Lord. But let's not forget that only a few weeks after Jesus washed His disciples' feet, those same hands commissioned those same feet to take God's mission into the world. As participants in Habitat for Humanity constantly remind themselves: "Give a hand up, not a handout".[31]

When we complete a hope-building project, our goal is that participants declare: "We did this!"

QUESTIONS TO PONDER:

1. What biblical principle for hope-building was evident from the placement of workers in rebuilding Jerusalem's walls?
2. What is "toxic charity"? When does our response to human need become toxic?
3. Do you recognize ways that your generosity might rob people of dignity?
4. How could your efforts to assist others help them take responsibility for their own welfare?

DAY 17

RALLY IDEALISTIC OUTSIDERS

Treasure the impact of distant partnerships:

The men of Jericho worked alongside them …. and…the Tekoites.

Melatiah the Gibeonite, Jadon the Meronothite, and the men of Gibeon and Mizpah, which was under the rule of the governor from across the Euphrates, worked alongside them.

The Valley Gate was rebuilt by Hanun and villagers of Zanoah.

After him came Nehemiah son of Azbuk, mayor of half the district of Beth Zur. He worked from just in front of the Tomb of David….

Nehemiah 3:2a, 5a, 7, 13a, 16a, MSG

Buried in Nehemiah's detailed account of wall-building are easy-to-miss hope-building principles. One of these axioms is the wisdom of involving partners who won't directly benefit from the endeavor but who aspire to advance God's reign.

We are told that the burden of reconstruction was shared by workers from Jericho (16 miles east), Tekoa (11 miles south), Gibeon (8 miles northwest), and Mizpah (8 mile west). It was several days walk from Jerusalem to Zanoah, Beth Zur, and Keilah (See Nehemiah 3:17). Jerusalem's walls would offer scant protection to these Jews when enemies attacked. Indeed, the wall rebuilding effort would alarm enemies, raising the risk of attack. Instead of clear-cut self-interest, Jews in the Judean countryside took risks and made sacrifices to restore the prominence of their faith. Jerusalem's restoration would demonstrate Yahweh's power to the nations. As the Lord proclaimed through the prophet in exile:

I am going to bring it recovery and healing; I will heal them and reveal to them abundance of prosperity and security. I will restore the fortunes of Judah and the fortunes of Israel, and rebuild them as they were at first. I will cleanse them from all the guilt of their sin against me, and I will forgive all the guilt of their sin and rebellion against me. And this city shall be to me a name of joy, a praise and a glory before all the nations of the earth who shall hear of all the good that I do for them; they shall fear and tremble because of all the good and all the prosperity I provide for it.   Jeremiah 33:6-9

In rallying Jews to rebuild their capital, Yahweh made His reign visible. Their restoration would be a sign of divine redemptive activity.

It is easy to rally self-interested people. It is more challenging to motivate those who aren't directly affected. Yet hope-builders recognize that abundant resources become available as we help outsiders imagine how their participation could advance the common good and make God's reign visible. This awareness is crucial, for hope-building work usually requires greater resources than what is available from those in proximity. Perhaps the work is too demanding for locals to do it alone. Maybe an insufficient number of those in proximity recognize their self-interest. God's purposes often necessitate involving partners who do not benefit, other than rejoicing in seeing God's reign manifested tangibly.

VISION CASTING YIELDS GENEROUS OUTSIDERS

The Apostle Paul was brilliant at drawing God's people into long-distance partnerships. In its early decades, the church in Jerusalem faced great hardship. Having sent apostles to share the gospel throughout the Empire, the remnant in Jerusalem struggled with persecution and famine. As he concluded his first letter to the Corinthians, Paul gave instructions for the collection of funds to feed believers in Jerusalem. In later correspondence, Paul portrayed this endeavor as more than a humanitarian project. Celebrating the exemplary giving of the Macedonians in northern Greece, Paul praised Jesus' power to unite strangers into an empire-wide family:

> We want you to know, brothers and sisters, about the grace of God that was given to the churches of Macedonia: During a severe trial brought about by affliction, their abundant joy and their extreme poverty overflowed in a wealth of generosity on their part. I can testify that, according to their ability and even beyond their ability, of their own accord, they begged us earnestly for the privilege of sharing in the ministry to the saints, and not just as we had hoped. Instead, they gave themselves first to the Lord and then to us by God's will.
>
> 2 Corinthians 8:1-5, CSB

Whether your hope-building requires greater funding or additional volunteers, it's likely that God wants to incorporate outside partners. Perhaps you involved several partners in the early stages as you "leveraged your assets" by "making asks." Some of these initial partners might give more as they discover that the intended beneficiaries are becoming invested. Other outsiders won't jump on board till the proverbial "train leaves the station." The key issue is whether these outside donors can see the move of God in your work.

During my first pastorate, our small congregation embarked on a capital campaign to build a sanctuary. Sixty families were challenged with significant "faith-raising." Our fundraising capacity seemed limited. Few of the households were financially comfortable. Located just northwest of Atlanta's I-285 Perimeter, our neighborhoods struggled with "white flight" and racial transition. While the congregation adapted marvelously—growing in size and diversity—raising funds for a new sanctuary seemed foolhardy. That's when the Lord sent a brother and sister who were partners in commercial property development. He had been the co-founder of a wildly successful upscale apartment franchise. The two of them sensed God's call to invest their wealth and skill into creating affordable and supportive apartment communities for young families. After hearing of our building program, he made a significant contribution and became an ongoing donor to our ministry budget, enabling us to hire a part-time youth pastor.

With God there is no shortage, for "Indeed, every animal of the forest is mine, even the cattle on a thousand hills" (Psalm 50:10, ISV). God will provide in surprising ways when we demonstrate our trust in His provision.

OUTSIDERS WHO COME TO SERVE

Fundraising partners can be easier to cultivate than servant leaders who give their time. (Were the men from Jericho and Tekoa tempted to send a check?)

After Lynn and I relocated our residence into a disadvantaged neighborhood, we took small steps to be a missional presence. We prayed over possibilities with a young couple who lived nearby, but they lost interest. We were alone...till God provided a middle-class couple who lived in our former community, near the beach. These friends sensed God's call to cross the causeway and build relationships in our working-class neighborhood—especially significant because she was the guidance counselor at the elementary school in our neighborhood.

You would think that the last place that an overworked school guidance counselor would want to focus her missional energy would be in the neighborhood where she already worked fifty hours a week. But this servant-hearted partner had a deep yearning to support the single mothers of her school. She and her husband were crucial as Lynn and I made our missional outreach in our neighborhood. When families came to our cookouts and block parties, she welcomed the children by name. She was tireless in organizing children's games. At our first cookout, she brought buckets of water balloons.

When I think of that couple, driving across the bridge to cultivate a missional community, I remember again: "When God gives vision, God also gives provision."

QUESTIONS TO PONDER:

1. How might serving in a hope-building endeavor benefit an outsider to that community?
2. How should partners from the outside take care not to sabotage hope-building efforts?
3. What aspects of your hope-building dreams would benefit from outside partners?

DAY 18

INVOLVE EVERYONE

Include everyone.

Taking a look at the people listed in Nehemiah chapter 3, we notice another theme: Nehemiah's hope-building project involved nearly everyone, including those normally excused from manual labor. There were skilled craftsmen who didn't view wall building labor as beneath their dignity:

> Uzziel son of Harhaiah of the goldsmiths' guild worked next to him, and next to him Hananiah, one of the perfumers. They rebuilt the wall of Jerusalem as far as the Broad Wall.   Nehemiah 3:8, MSG

Despite the patriarchal mindset, women's contributions were recognized:

> Working next to him was Shallum son of Hallohesh, mayor of the other half-district of Jerusalem, along with his daughters.
> Nehemiah 3:12, MSG

Even religious professionals and a civic official toiled under the hot sun:

> Levites under Rehum son of Bani were next in line. Alongside them, Hashabiah, mayor of half the district of Keilah, represented his district in the rebuilding...priests from the neighborhood went on from there.   Nehemiah 3:17, 22, MSG

Remarkable hope-building happens when leaders rally the whole community to give their best. In 1910, a fire destroyed the wood frame building used by First (African American) Baptist Church of Montgomery, Alabama. Because the congregation was comprised of low-income families, Pastor Andrew Stokes challenged the members of the congregation to find and bring a brick to each Sunday service. What became known as the "Brick-A-Day" church was completed in 1916.

In the years that followed, First Baptist Church swelled to 5,000 members, the largest black Baptist congregation in the United States at its peak. As a frequent gathering spot for civil rights demonstrators, the brick structure survived a bombing in 1957. On the night of May 21, 1961, the nation's attention was drawn to that same facility when 3,000 white vigilantes threatened to burn it down as it hosted the Freedom Riders. Only when President Kennedy federalized the Alabama National Guard was catastrophe prevented. [32] One cannot help but reflect on the many ways that this hope-built structure was a sanctuary for hope.

GO FAR TOGETHER!

An African proverb reminds us that "if you want to go fast, travel alone; but if you want to go far, go together."[33] Resist the temptation to think that "if I want it done right, I must do it myself." Those who lead should invest their energies into preparing others for hope-building. While we do well to shoulder some of the work as role models, we do better to train and mentor others to share the load. Not only are we more likely to get the work done, involving others provides huge social benefits.

Few organizations rally diverse people more effectively than Habitat for Humanity. Partner families in need of affordable housing toil alongside volunteers from every imaginable walk of life. When our congregation took responsibility for constructing three Habitat homes, hundreds of church members stepped up to serve. Alongside qualifying partner families were experienced tradesmen, do-it-yourselfers, and at tasks they usually paid others to perform. *Shared vision forges diverse and disconnected people into hope-building partners.*

As we've been reminded, when God calls us into hope-building, God also leads us to build community. Restoring God's reign on earth has the effect of strengthening relationships and furthering "the ministry of reconciliation" (2 Corinthians 5:18, CSB). God's Kingdom becomes visible when God's work builds bridges between people who are otherwise separated by race, income, social class, or ideology.

INVOLVE UNDER-RESOURCED PEOPLE

This bias to involve everyone in service not only motivates us to recruit the affluent, it also compels us to invite under-resourced people to contribute money as they are able. Jesus' parable of the "Widow's Mite" (Luke 21:1-3) reminds us that the poor should not be denied the opportunity to worship God by giving a portion of their income. Including them affirms their dignity and cultivates responsibility. The Apostle Paul celebrated how the Macedonian Christians "extreme poverty overflowed in a wealth of generosity" (2 Corinthians 8:2, CSB).

When our small, Atlanta-area congregation engaged in "faith-raising" fundraising, we sent carefully trained visiting stewards to our members' homes, to ask for three-year financial commitments. To meet our goal, we challenged each other to dedicate an additional three percent of our income to the congregation's building program.

In the week prior, I prayed over the difficult task of assigning names to pairs of these visiting stewards. Generally, I matched people who already knew each other. I also arranged for people to visit with those of a similar level of income, but I wondered about a woman named Patsy. Should we include her? Patsy and her seven children lived in a subsidized apartment just a few blocks from the church building. Her family didn't own a car. They began to worship with us after we provided van rides to anyone seeking transportation to worship. It was apparent to me that they were dependent on governmental assistance.

Could we ask a single mom with seven children to commit funds to a capital campaign? Or should we assume that she couldn't afford to give? After much prayer, I sensed that Patsy should be included, even if our church members felt uncomfortable asking her for money

I decided to visit her myself, and she was ready! I handed her the pledge card. She filled it out, declaring her intention to donate an appropriate amount each month for three years. It gave her great satisfaction to help build that sanctuary. Hope-building involves *everyone*.

QUESTIONS TO PONDER:

1. What details from Nehemiah 3 indicate the amazing degree to which non-construction workers joined with laborers to rebuild the stone walls of Jerusalem?
2. In your own hope-building project, what circumstances would make it appropriate to invite everyone involved to make a sacrificial effort?
3. In what situations do people seem most willing to "roll up their sleeves" for the kind of work that they usually avoid?

CULTIVATE SERVANTS' HEARTS

Hope-building cultivates Christ-like character.

Sustained hope-building requires teams of people who are willing and able to do the work. Although this is a tall order, God can transform self-centered people into disciples of Jesus who derive joy from serving God's larger purposes, especially when used to bless others. Sometimes God will provide ministry partners who already generous, humble, cooperative, and coachable. Far more common is the necessity that we help others mature as they participate in hope-building.

While utilizing "self-help" resources cultivates personal growth, the impact of our Lord's sacrificial love can be immeasurably transformative. For eleven chapters, Paul's letter to the Romans celebrates the game-changing news that Jesus' death on the cross makes sinners righteous in God's eyes. No longer would people need to atone for sin by offering animals as costly sacrifices. Neither need modern people engage in futile attempts to make themselves worthy. The message of the cross provides the opportunity for a gracious exchange: we give Jesus our sin; Jesus grants us his righteousness.

As the twelfth chapter begins, Paul pivots to how we should respond to this good news:

> Therefore, brothers and sisters, in view of the mercies of God, I urge you to present your bodies as a living sacrifice, holy and pleasing to God; this is your true worship. Do not be conformed to this age, but be transformed by the renewing of your mind, so that you may discern what is the good, pleasing, and perfect will of God.
>
> Romans 12:1-2, CSB

LIVING SACRIFICE

This powerful experience of God's grace yields deep gratitude. Worship is no longer is confined to Sunday services. Daily life takes on a whole new dimension. Yearning to please God and advance God's work, each day we offer our bodies as a "living sacrifice."

Yet there's a problem with living sacrifices: they can "crawl off the altar![34] Until we receive our heavenly reward, we wrestle with the temptation not to be living sacrifices. To sustain God-honoring lives, each day's choices reflect our determination that we "not conform to the pattern of this world" (narcissism and self-centeredness). The encouraging news is that those who continually welcome God's gracious influence are "transformed by the renewing of your mind," and we become people who actually enjoy sacrificial service, a beautiful aspect of God's "good, pleasing, and perfect will."

Recognizing that a detailed description of "living sacrifice" would be helpful to the church, Paul painted a word-portrait of servant-heartedness:

> For by the grace given to me, I tell everyone among you not to think of himself more highly than he should think. Instead, think sensibly, as God has distributed a measure of faith to each one. Now as we have many parts in one body, and all the parts do not have the same function, in the same way we who are many are one body in Christ and individually members of one another.   Romans 12:3-5, CSB

Your hope-building calling provides the opportunity to be a "living sacrifice" and to cultivate this identity in others. As you strive to build hope, let God use you to build character in people. Model humility. Call them away from individualism that avoids commitment. Demonstrate your conviction that God wants to act as "one body in Christ and individually members of one other" (Rom. 12:5, CSB). In Paul's context, churches were citywide networks of "house churches." "One body" refers primarily to the Christ-followers with whom you share life's journey. Not only seek to know others; allow yourself to be known by them. By sharing your lives, we "carry one another's burdens; in this way...fulfill the law of Christ" (Galatians 6:2). This intimate spiritual fellowship of hope-building partners is a "family on mission...integrating family and mission into one life."[35]

SHARE ADVENTUROUS FAITH

A family on mission will benefit from synergy as God provides its members with complementary gifts. As participants make daily choices that reflect their desire to be "living sacrifices," they benefit from "iron sharpens iron" fellowship as they advance God's mission (Proverbs 27:17).

Gently but firmly, we need to encourage each other to "stay on the altar." Here's how we cultivate the shift from "self-centeredness" to "sacrificial living:"

1. Feed each other God's Word. Don't only consume feel-good writings, the spiritual equivalent of processed carbohydrates designed to yield a "sugar high." Use Bible study opportunities to feast upon the scriptural equivalent of meat and vegetables.

2. Cultivate communities that provide Christ-followers with the opportunity to experience the adventure of sharing God's mission. Missional communities, outwardly focused life groups, and mutually supportive ministry teams have great potential of becoming families on mission. [36]

3. In your personal prayer life, intercede for your brothers and sisters by name, God can use servant-hearted Christ-followers to influence less spiritually mature believers. One of the potential benefits of authentic Christian community is that because of their proximity, "living sacrifice" Christ-followers inevitably help "baby believers" recognize the otherwise-hidden idols that hinder their growth.

A Roman Catholic layman looms large among the servant-hearted volunteers who have crossed my path. Wendell is a retired Air Force colonel who helped to organize the East Central Florida chapter of Kairos, an ecumenical prison ministry. Kairos conducts behind-bars weekend spiritual renewal retreats. After years of befriending and sharing his faith with convicts, Wendell sensed God's call to become a tutor for disadvantaged children in hopes of preventing the waste of lives in crime and incarceration.

After hearing about the DOCK's after-school program in the Booker T. Washington Neighborhood, Wendell became a weekly mentor. Not only did he help hundreds of children with their homework, Wendell also made a point of learning their names—a challenge because many of the African American children's names could sound unfamiliar to an older white man. It was common to see Wendell pull out a folded paper from his front shirt pocket to review his notes or add details, just so he could call each child by name.

Nothing builds hope like a "living sacrifice"!

QUESTIONS TO PONDER:

1. If Jesus Christ is the ultimate sacrifice, then why is each Christ-followers expected to be a "living sacrifice"?

2. What barriers(s) have discouraged you from a lifestyle of being a "living sacrifice?"

3. What benefits are received by members of a "family on mission"?

DAY 20

EQUIP OTHERS FOR SERVICE

We can't do it all.

The pursuit of hope-building increases the risk of burnout, especially if we attempt to do too much on our own, and members of our team let us down.

Have you heard the story about the peculiar pastor who served a small-town church? The congregation's historic edifice was in the heart of town, the corner of Elm and Main Streets. Each day in the late afternoon, the pastor left his study, walked to the parking lot, and opened the trunk of the car. Removing a lawn chair, he carried it to the nearby railroad crossing. There he sat, waiting in silence. At precisely 5:15 p.m., a train whistle blew in the distance. The crossing lights flashed, and the warning bells erupted. When the crossbar came down, the pastor stood expectantly. Within seconds, the massive locomotive roared by, blowing dust and leaves high into the air.

Then it would happen. As the freight cars raced by, the pastor began to cheer, "Yay!" He would leap towards the sky, arms extended overhead, shouting with joy as if he witnessed a game-winning touchdown.

This strange behavior became the talk of the town. Eventually, the church's elders requested a meeting. After asking why he made such a spectacle, the pastor explained:

> For ten years, I've been trying to lead the members of our church to reach out to neighbors, serve the poor, and share our faith. I've preached sermons, held training sessions, and organized service projects. A few people have helped, but rarely does anyone else take the initiative. The 5:15 freight train is the only thing that happens in this town without me pushing or pulling it!

Remembering that peculiar pastor helps me to laugh at myself when disappointments accumulate, cleansing my soul of toxicity. Oh Lord, don't let me end up cheering the passing train!

As we gain awareness that disappointment is breeding discouragement, it's crucial to renew the habits that foster emotional and spiritual health: exercise...devotionals...prayer...sharing burdens with trusted friends. Yet it's equally important to address the underlying reasons why nothing seems to happen "unless I push or pull it...." *So often, we've simply not learned effective ways to equip and deploy people for service.*

Taking the time and making the effort to involve people is as important as getting tasks done. Cultivating servant-heartedness will yield huge dividends. God promises to magnify the impact of our faithfulness. There's also a wondrous surprise. As we forge hope-building teams of servant-hearted people, we discover that the living Lord equips participants with spiritual gifts that enable each to contribute.

SPIRITUAL GIFTS

A servant-hearted mindset subverts our individualism and cultivates our capacity for genuine community. With humility we recognize that individual believers are "many parts in one body, and all the parts do not have the same function" for "according to the grace given to us, we have different gifts" (Romans 12:4, 6, CSB).

While the New Testament names at least nineteen spiritual gifts, Paul described five primary gifts as crucial for God's mission:

Now grace was given to each one of us according to the measure of Christ's gift...

And he himself gave some to be apostles, some prophets, some evangelists, some pastors and teachers, to equip the saints for the work of ministry, to build up the body of Christ, until we all reach unity in the faith and in the knowledge of God's Son, growing into maturity with a stature measured by Christ's fullness. Then we will no longer be little children, tossed by the waves and blown around by every wind of teaching, by human cunning with cleverness in the techniques of deceit. But speaking the truth in love, let us grow in every way into him who is the head—Christ. From him the whole body, fitted and knit together by every supporting ligament, promotes the growth of the body for building itself up in love by the proper working of each individual part.   Ephesians 4:7, 11-16, CSB

As you strive to establish hope-building teams, rejoice in Paul's assurance that the triune God works proactively. Not only does the Lord provide each person with a unique personality, distinct life-skills, wisdom-gleaning experience, and a unique testimony, the Holy Spirit also apportions to each the ability to function as an apostle, prophet, evangelist, shepherd, or teacher. Pioneers in the missional church movement have utilized a memory device called APEST.[37] Ideally, those sharing leadership are gifted to excel in these complementary functions:

Apostles: those who pioneer new missional effort by "sending and multiplying"

Prophets: those who are able to discern the spiritual realities of a given situation and to communicate them in a timely and appropriate manner to advance God's mission; also "calling out sin and challenging God's people to greater fidelity to God, his Word, and his ways"

Evangelists: while every disciple can share his/her faith journey and essentials of the Gospel, some are "naturally infectious" and are also gifted with the ability to communicate more effectively, so that even skeptics become disciples[38]

Shepherds/ Pastors: those who excel in caregiving, nurturing, encouraging, and protecting the people of God

Teachers: disciples supernaturally gifted in communicating the revealed wisdom of God so that the people of God learn to obey all that Christ has commanded

Church members often expect their pastor to excel in all five of these areas. Somehow, the word "pastor" came to mean a trained professional who does most of the ministry. In truth, many professional clergy have only minimal competence in certain areas. Therefore, ministry professionals are much more effective when they cultivate ministry leaders who utilize complementary gifts. Hope-building teams thrive when they provide an environment for participants to discover, claim, and exercise spiritual gifts, in order "to equip the saints for works of ministry" (Ephesians 4:12, CSB).

APPRENTICESHIP

Often the reluctance to take initiative is rooted in the fear of failure. Preparing God's people for ministry requires patience. Provide your hope-building partners with opportunities to take small steps that will lead to increased confidence, competence, and a willingness to shoulder greater responsibility and take personal initiative.

When asking a fellow team member to take a particular role, invite him or her to be your apprentice. Whether teaching others to lead in prayer, host a home gathering, lead a discussion of scripture, invite neighbors to a cookout, or send out a compelling email, this simple process will empower them:

I do; you watch.

I do; you help.

You do; I help.

You do; I watch.

Ideally this cycle ends with your apprentice finding his or her own apprentice. How much more impact we will make if we incorporate leadership reproduction into our hope-building.[39]

To have sufficient musicians to add satellite congregations, one multi-site church required its musicians to apprentice other musicians. In one memorable instance, I heard an experienced drummer describe his mentoring of a young musician. Yet when it was time for the third step (You do; I help), the young man wasn't quite ready to set the beat for the worship team. In most churches, such a novice wouldn't play till he was proficient. In that congregation, the apprentice drummer took his place on the stage with the experienced drummer crouched behind him, tapping the beat on his leg.[40]

Equip others as you build hope.

QUESTIONS TO PONDER:

1. What are the five primary spiritual gifts? How has the Lord equipped you to benefit and advance His mission? (There is a helpful online survey is at alanhirsch.org/tests.)

2. Think of the other Christ-followers who share God's work with you. How could you help them discern their spiritual giftedness? What tasks could you share with them?

3. Have you ever apprenticed anyone? Who could you invite to be your apprentice? What task or role could you offload if you apprentice effectively?

DAY 21

BRIDGES HAVE GUARDRAILS

God's people no longer build walls.

While following Nehemiah's city-securing odyssey informs and inspires, Jesus' followers were commissioned to "go and make disciples of all nations" (Matthew 28:19). Instead of erecting bulwarks against danger, the Apostles trusted God to make them dangerous to powers and principalities as they entered Greco-Roman cities with the liberating message of grace.

BRIDGES NOT WALLS

The Gospel of Jesus brings down walls of separation. Despite the religious and cultural alienation that kept Jews and Gentiles in separate spheres, Paul announced that Jesus "is our peace, who made both groups one and tore down the dividing wall of hostility" (Ephesians 2:14, CSB). To the Gentiles, Paul declared that "you are no longer foreigners and strangers, but fellow citizens with the saints, and members of God's household" (Ephesians 2:19, CSB).

Hope-building compels Christ-followers to build bridges. Yet as bridges have guard rails to prevent travelers from falling into an abyss, hope-building safeguards protect teams from veering dangerously off course. Bridge-building strategies require boundary-setting tactics.

BOUNDARIES NONETHELESS

Hope-building safeguards begin with common sense boundaries, showing how team members treat each other and relate to the community. Theological guardrails are crucial when building bridges that connect people to God. When reading the New Testament, we discover that it's not our bodies, but the essentials of our faith, that most need protection. As Paul appealed to Timothy:

> Hold on to the pattern of sound teaching that you have heard from me, in the faith and love that are in Christ Jesus. Guard the good deposit through the Holy Spirit who lives in us.
>
> 2 Timothy 1:13-14, CSB

Near the end of the first century, the Revelation to John asserted the importance of theological guardrails. The risen Lord commended His church in Ephesus because "[they] have tested those who call themselves apostles, but are not, and have found them to be false" (Revelation 2:2, ISV).

In the centuries that followed, waves of false teaching threatened the church's core convictions. "Gnostic gospels" that distorted the mystery of the Incarnation went viral. To preserve the orthodox message of hope, a series of church councils set boundaries. Certain gospels and epistles were affirmed as the Canon (rule) of scripture while others were deemed heretical. The Nicene and Chalcedonian councils crafted creeds, which became the written summaries of core Christian teaching.

In every generation, the church universal wrestles with the never-ending task of communicating clear boundaries to protect Jesus' disciples from the risk of veering off the bridges they seek to build. To preserve the truth, ensure that those who lead the Christian communities commit to remain within such guardrails.

BOUNDARIES IGNORED

I've served on committees that examined ministerial candidates for readiness prior to their ordination. It was inspiring to hear men and women chronicle their faith journeys and share their sense of call. In most cases, the intellectual and emotional rigors of seminary study deepened their faith and forged strong, biblically based convictions. Yet several times the committee was approached by candidates who didn't seem ready for ordination; they lacked confidence in the authority of scripture and the lordship of Christ.

In one case, a candidate for ordination answered a question in this manner: "Jesus is my Lord, but I cannot say that he is 'the Lord.'" Follow-up questions revealed that she viewed Jesus's lordship as a personal choice rather than a universal reality. After she left the room, a debate ensued as to whether she was ready for ordination. Two of us appealed to the other three committee members to wait until she could fully affirm Jesus' singular, saving lordship.

Insisting that church leaders embrace foundational doctrines might seem negative. Nonetheless, these difficult conversations are crucial in preserving the church's hope-building message. Leaders can fulfill Paul's admonition to "guard the good deposit" if they hold fast to the truth of the gospel (2 Timothy 1:14, CSB). In the next chapter, Paul reminded the younger pastor if the DNA of the gospel remained undiluted and undistorted, it would be viral. Alluding to five subsequent generations of gospel multiplication, Paul wrote: "What **you** have heard from **me** through **many witnesses** entrust to **faithful people** who will be able to **teach others** as well" (2 Timothy 2:2, IJV—each distinct generation emphasized with bold text).

Gospel clarity inspires and energizes Christ-followers to build bridges that take them into unknown terrain. *As roadway bridges need guardrails, sharing Jesus through relational bridges requires boundaries of belief.* Strong in our gospel-centered identity, we dare to engage and befriend people who don't yet share our convictions.

QUESTIONS TO PONDER:

1. Might your hope-building team benefit by naming assumed standards of behavior?
2. Does it matter whether the core leaders of your group share faith convictions and theological boundaries?
3. How might you prepare yourself for opportunities to share what and why you believe?

WEEK 4

OVERCOME OPPOSITION

Previously we discovered that Nehemiah's channeling of holy discontent stirred up unholy discontent among those people or groups who victimized God's people. This resistance to positive change will erupt into an escalating series of attacks, each one intended to stop God's people from rebuilding Jerusalem's walls and restoring the city's vitality.

Good deeds sometimes provoke evil responses. Attacks can be fierce. Sometimes they compromise or halt our hope-building. But unlike the physical properties described in Newton's "Third Law of Motion," evil's response to good is not an "equal and opposite reaction."[41] In the long run, evil cannot thwart God's ultimate will for humanity. As Martin Luther King Jr. famously declared, "the arc of the moral universe is long, but it bends toward justice."[42] Reading Nehemiah reminds us that God's good is more powerful than evil, for God is actively working to redeem and restore humanity. Jesus' resurrection confirmed that light and life will prevail.

In the meantime, hope-building requires us to engage in spiritual warfare. Nehemiah's faithful response to opponents can teach us much about fighting evil without allowing evil to overtake our hearts. As Paul urged the Romans, "overcome evil with good" (Romans 12:21).

DAY 22

SELF-AWARE PRAYER

Prayer is our greatest weapon for good, as long as we don't delude ourselves.

Now when Sanballat heard that we were building the wall, he was angry and greatly enraged, and he mocked the Jews. He said in the presence of his associates and of the army of Samaria, "What are these feeble Jews doing? Will they restore things? Will they sacrifice? Will they finish it in a day? Will they revive the stones out of the heaps of rubbish—and burned ones at that?" Tobiah the Ammonite was beside him, and he said, "That stone wall they are building—any fox going up on it would break it down!" Hear, O our God, for we are despised; turn their taunt back on their own heads, and give them over as plunder in a land of captivity. Do not cover their guilt, and do not let their sin be blotted out from your sight; for they have hurled insults in the face of the builders.

So we rebuilt the wall, and all the wall was joined together to half its height; for the people had a mind to work.   Nehemiah 4:1-6

On days 11 and 13 we learned of Sanballat and Tobiah's initial attempt to derail Nehemiah's hope-building (Nehemiah 2:19-20). Now we read that Sanballat "became angry and was greatly incensed" (Neh. 4:1a). The Samaritan general and his allies were furious that their ridicule had not deterred God's people from working in harmony. Neither had Sanballat's accusation of disloyalty to the Persian king shaken Nehemiah's confidence that God would protect and provide.

The wall was nearly half-finished. Recognizing that Jerusalem could soon defend itself, its enemies ramped up their opposition. This time Sanballat tried to demoralize the entire population. With troops as a backdrop, he taunted the Jews, questioning their stamina and wall-building skills. Especially insulting was Tobiah's snarky suggestion that a fox would topple their work.

SPIRITUAL WARFARE

Initially, these taunts were ineffective, but Sanballat's attacks would take their toll. Extended labor makes people vulnerable to doubts, disharmony, and deceit. Ever the perceptive leader, Nehemiah recognized their weakness. Despite reassuring signs that sturdy walls were being rebuilt rapidly, he took these new threats seriously. Again, Nehemiah took up his primary weapon: prayer. The greatest resource for hope-building leaders is God's favor. In his prayer, with raw vulnerability, Nehemiah entrusted the disheartening situation to the Lord: "turn their taunt back on their own heads, and give them over as plunder in a land of captivity." (4:4).

God's response to Nehemiah's prayer was to unite the workers in their work. For the moment, the people of Jerusalem were undistracted. As Nehemiah reported: "So we rebuilt the wall, and all the wall was joined together to half its height; for the people had a mind to work" (Neh. 4:6).

Prayer didn't eliminate Nehemiah's problems. The opposition would intensify. God's favor didn't protect His people from setbacks. There are more drama and faith lessons to come.

Conflicts are inevitable. Hope-building increases the possibility that unseen spiritual forces will subvert our efforts to bless. While human beings may embody the threat, authentic prayer recognizes that "our struggle is not against enemies of blood and flesh, but against the rulers, against the authorities, against the cosmic powers of this present darkness, against the spiritual forces of evil in the heavenly places" (Ephesians 6:12.) These dark powers are most destructive when they persuade people (including us) to delude ourselves.

UNAWARE PRAYER

Prayer yields positive outcomes when conversation with God heightens our self-awareness. When praying people repent of sin and become like Christ, God-honoring projects are more likely to be completed, broken lives more frequently healed, and conflicts tend to be diffused.

I cherish many memories of redemption and reconciliation, yet I also bear witness to a catastrophe. After twenty years as a senior pastor, I became caught in an intractable conflict with some of my staff colleagues and several elders. Like Nehemiah, we prayed for divine intervention, sometimes praying together. But half-hearted attempts to dialogue and reconcile went nowhere. In retrospect, I suspect that aspects of our prayers were self-deluded.

The conflict festered because we were blind to our faults. I viewed myself as a fair, collegial, and approachable senior pastor. Yet several staff colleagues perceived me as a dominating bully. Clearly, I needed to hear and heed their complaints. Anticipating such situations, Jesus instructed the church:

> If your brother sins against you, go and confront him while the two of you are alone. If he listens to you, you have won back your brother. But if he doesn't listen, take one or two others with you so that 'every word may be confirmed by the testimony of two or three witnesses.'"
> Matthew 18:15-16, ISV

Many of us involved didn't recognize our own brokenness and blindness. Some colleagues disobeyed Jesus' clear-cut teaching on conflict resolution. Whether due to passive-aggressive emotions or ulterior motives, people I counted as friends would not tell me how I had offended them. They resorted to secret meetings and composed a damning narrative of exaggerated, out-of-context allegations. Several church elders became accomplices. Listening to allegations without hearing the "other side" inevitably yields bias.

The catastrophe was nearly averted after eight tense months. Our governing board of pastors and elders voted unanimously to engage in a biblically based conflict-resolution process. Professional Christian mediators would interview the staff and elder board to determine which parties needed reconciliation. Active listening and coaching would prepare us for conflict-resolution conversations. The goal was to cultivate empathetic listening, self-awareness, sincere repentance, authentic reconciliation, and renewed gospel partnership.

Yet as Sanballat was unrelenting against Jerusalem, Satan worked nonstop to hinder the path to reconciliation. Just before the conflict-resolution process was to commence, my estranged staff colleagues convinced elder allies to postpone the peacemaking mediation. Denominational leaders assumed that they could ascertain the truth without a full investigation. Instead of giving me an opportunity to respond to allegations, the regional authorities simply interviewed those who made anonymous complaints and concluded that I had abused my authority. Though the counselor appointed by denominational leaders recommended that the conflict-resolution process resume, I was forced to resign. Six months later, my accusers were compelled to resign when conflict escalated after my departure.

The catastrophe might have been avoided had we engaged in self-aware prayer. I share this painful experience in hopes that you can avoid self-deception. The unraveling of relationships accelerated after I foolishly confronted a staff colleague in front of the governing board. Previously, I had prayed for guidance, but in retrospect, I had deluded myself into believing that the Spirit had led me to confront him. Had I sounded out a trusted friend or my wife, the Lord could have used him or her to warn me of self-deception.

Although they prayed for direction, those estranged from me chose not to heed Jesus' teaching in Matthew 18, nor did the denominational officials support biblically based conflict-resolution.

SELF-AWARE PRAYER

Because we are sinners, prayer can be sincere AND self-deluding. The Arbinger Institute portrays this self-delusion as being "in a box":

Self-deception is like this. It blinds us to the true causes of problems, and once we're blind, all the "solutions" we can think of will actually make matters worse. Whether at work or at home, self-deception obscures the truth about ourselves, corrupts our view of others and our circumstances, and inhibits our ability to make wise and helpful decisions.[43]

By contrast, self-aware prayer has these characteristics:

1. **Humility:** We recognize our tendency to be self-deluded about our lingering brokenness. Instead of using prayer as a religious cover to rationalize unhealthy behavior, we ask the Lord to make us more aware of hidden motives and give us the strength to repent, forgive, and reconcile.
2. **Revelation**: Instead of relying upon the world's ways, which often manipulates people or misuses institutional power to silence, separate, and scapegoat people, we search the Bible for divine wisdom that fosters mutual repentance and reconciliation.
3. **Reliance**: As we strive to honor God with our actions, we trust in God's protection. The Sovereign One may vindicate our cause, or God may choose to use our suffering for a greater redemptive purpose, as demonstrated in the death and resurrection of Jesus.

Despite painful losses, the Lord has been healing my heart and reshaping me for missional leadership. The difference is this: like an Old Testament patriarch, I now "lead with a limp."[44] After wrestling with God, Jacob the manipulator faced his estranged brother Esau; Jacob was weaker and limped now. Yet with vulnerability came the opportunity to rely upon God, humble himself, reconcile with his brother, and become "Israel," an anointed leader serving God's redemptive purpose (Genesis 32-33). I lead best when I acknowledge the limp that lingers from my painful past.

Conflict is inevitable. Hope-building increases the risk and raises the stakes. Strive to be self-aware. *Acknowledge your own imperfections with the people you lead*. In your actions, heed God's Word. Rely on God's protection as you face your vulnerability.

QUESTIONS TO PONDER:

1. Have you experienced catastrophic conflicts, despite prayers for better outcomes?
2. What are ways that prayer can be self-deluded?
3. Which of the named characteristics of "self-aware prayer" are helpful to you?

DAY 23

WHEN EVIL THREATENS HARM

Sometimes building hope makes God's people more vulnerable.

But when Sanballat and Tobiah and the Arabs and the Ammonites and the Ashdodites heard that the repairing of the walls of Jerusalem was going forward and the gaps were beginning to be closed, they were very angry, and all plotted together to come and fight against Jerusalem and to cause confusion in it. So we prayed to our God, and set a guard as a protection against them day and night.

But Judah said, "The strength of the burden bearers is failing, and there is too much rubbish so that we are unable to work on the wall." And our enemies said, "They will not know or see anything before we come upon them and kill them and stop the work." When the Jews who lived near them came, they said to us ten times, "From all the places where they live they will come up against us."

Nehemiah 4:7-12

Sanballat forged a fearsome alliance, uniting the non-Jewish population against Jerusalem's restoration: Samaritans to the north, Arabs to the south, Ammonites to the east, and the people of Ashdod (technologically superior Philistines) to the west. After attempts to demoralize the wall builders failed, the threat level increased, for "they were very angry, all plotted together to come and fight against Jerusalem" (Neh. 4:7b).

Again, Nehemiah and his colleagues "prayed to our God" (4:9a). This time, he took prudent action, posting a guard around the clock. Yet strengthening the city's defenses didn't shore up its residents' confidence. Wall building exhausted them: "The strength of the burden bearers is failing, and there is too much rubbish so that we are unable to work on the wall" (4:10b). Fear overwhelmed them: Their enemies were overheard to say that the Jews "will not know or see anything before we come upon them and kill them and stop the work." (4:11). Hysteria was palpable as Judah's men were told "ten times, `from all the places where they live they will come up against us'" (4:12b).

The next section of Nehemiah will report that after several days, people "returned to the wall" when their leader addressed their fears (4:15). For several days, Jerusalem's enemies succeeded in thwarting the hope-building. Though the walls were halfway built, intimidation tactics persuaded the fearful and exhausted Jews to halt. Fear and exhaustion can be a paralyzing combination.

PROTECTION AGAINST UNRESTRAINED FEAR

In the depths of the Great Depression, President Roosevelt famously declared that "the only thing we have to fear is fear itself."[45] Unrestrained fear magnifies danger. Fear-filled people act to the detriment of their self-interest. Why else would Jerusalem's residents cease to build walls designed to protect them from enemies?

Fear can also tempt our teams to abandon their hope-building. Most common is the fear of shortage. We can be preoccupied—even immobilized—by concerns that we won't have enough time, energy, skill, money, or volunteers to sustain the effort. *The remedy is always prayer.* We go to our knees, for the Lord has declared that "every animal of the forest is mine, even the cattle on a thousand hills" (Psalm 50:10, ISV). It's when we are most stretched that God often chooses to provide richly, in concert with our prayer.

As we pray, the Lord often renews vision. As the Spirit reveals refreshing glimpses of God's preferred future, our energy is restored. As the prophet declared, "those who wait upon the LORD shall renew their strength" (Isaiah 40:31). As we recall God's promises in scripture, we are reminded that our Lord "can do infinitely more than all we can ask or imagine according to the power that is working among us" (Ephesians 3:20, ISV). Sharing refreshed vision rekindles the flame of hope and ignites the passion needed to impact our world. Prayer-infused vision casting is one way that God's people complete the "good works, which God prepared ahead of time for us to do" (Ephesians 2:10, CSB). Where God guides, God will provide. When God gives vision, God also gives provision. Don't fear shortage!

Some hope-builders face danger. Being called into God's mission can increase physical risk. Distributing food or providing healthcare during a pandemic might expose you to the possibility of infection. Venturing into a troubled neighborhood or an impoverished nation may increase your exposure to crime. Opponents of a community-blessing project might resort to intimidation tactics. Sustained hope-building may require us to face our fears

FACING GUNMEN WHILE SPIRITUALLY ARMED

In 2010, Dave and Becky Helsby were raising seven children while leading an orphanage west of Lake Victoria in Tanzania. One night the phone rang. A neighboring family reported the terrifying news that three men with a gun were beating on the door. Within moments they were inside the house, firing the gun and beating the father. After the phone went dead, Dave drove to their driveway and blew his horn to distract the robbers. The men ran outside, enabling the mother and children to lock themselves in the bathroom. Jumping out of the car, Dave took cover as shots were fired in his direction. He hid in tall grass and made his way back to his family's home. When the robbers showed up at his house, Becky and the children prayed fervently as Dave led them to the office. After Dave gave them heavy bags of coins, the robbers emptied his backpack to make room for the coins, not realizing that in their rush they had dumped out an envelope of bills with far greater value. Looking back on the experience, it's remarkable that the injuries weren't worse and the losses greater.

For many more years, the Helsbys remained in Tanzania, emerging from the trauma with deeper awareness of God's attentive care for servants who trust Him. While not guaranteeing personal security, the Lord's providential hand often spares us the worst. Even if we suffer, the scriptures remind us that God is in control, using our disappointments and failures to magnify our influence for redemptive purposes.

DANGEROUS TO EVIL

Nehemiah's experience reminds us not to be foolish when facing shortage or physical threats. Neither should we be so foolish as to miss the opportunity to be used by God to bless others. Jesus said that whoever wants "to save their life will lose it, and those who lose their life for my sake, and for the sake of the gospel, will save it" (Mark 8:35). Responding to the popular Christian myth that the "safest place is in the center of God's will," Erwin McManus wrote,

> The truth of the matter is that the center of God's will is not a safe place but the most dangerous place in the world! God fears nothing and no one! God moves with intentionality and power. To live outside of God's will put us in danger, to live in his will makes us dangerous.[46]

While our fears are undeniable, the evil, unjust powers and principalities have more to fear, for we claim the name of Jesus and bear the Holy Spirit. Our fears can be vanquished by our risen Lord. He has promised: "...I am with you always, to the end of the age" (Matthew 28:20). His powerful presence calms His children: "Peace I leave with you. My peace I give to you. I do not give to you as the world gives. Don't let your heart be troubled or fearful" (John 14:27, CSB). Reflecting on how he faced his fears, the Apostle Paul wrote:

> Who can separate us from the love of Christ? Can affliction or distress or persecution or famine or nakedness or danger or sword?...

No, in all these things we are more than conquerors through him who loved us. For I am persuaded that neither death nor life, nor angels nor rulers, nor things present nor things to come, nor powers, nor height nor depth, nor any other created thing will be able to separate us from the love of God that is in Christ Jesus our Lord.

Romans 8:35, 37-39, CSB

QUESTIONS TO PONDER:

1. Have you ever participated in a ministry situation or a mission trip that placed you at risk of physical or emotional harm? What practical measures were undertaken to protect you? Did the experience also help you to trust in God?
2. Are there aspects to your current calling that raise the risk of harm? How can you be prudent in protecting yourself without violating your commitment to honor our Lord Jesus Christ?

DAY 24

OUR BEST DEFENSE

Spirituality doesn't yield complacency. When confronted with the harsh reality that his enemies' intimidation succeeded in bringing a work stoppage, Nehemiah rose to action.

So in the lowest parts of the space behind the wall, in open places, I stationed the people according to their families, with their swords, their spears, and their bows. After I looked these things over, I stood up and said to the nobles and the officials and the rest of the people, "Do not be afraid of them. Remember the Lord, who is great and awesome, and fight for your kin, your sons, your daughters, your wives, and your homes."

When our enemies heard that their plot was known to us, and that God had frustrated it, we all returned to the wall, each to his work. From that day on, half of my servants worked on construction, and half held the spears, shields, bows, and body-armor; and the leaders posted themselves behind the whole house of Judah, who were building the wall. The burden bearers carried their loads in such a way that each labored on the work with one hand and with the other held a weapon. And each of the builders had his sword strapped at his side while he built. The man who sounded the trumpet was beside me. And I said to the nobles, the officials, and the rest of the people, "The work is great and widely spread out, and we are separated far from one another on the wall. Rally to us wherever you hear the sound of the trumpet. Our God will fight for us."

So we labored at the work, and half of them held the spears from break of dawn until the stars came out. I also said to the people at that time, "Let every man and his servant pass the night inside Jerusalem, so that they may be a guard for us by night and may labor by day." So neither I nor my brothers nor my servants nor the men of the guard who followed me ever took off our clothes; each kept his weapon in his right hand.   Nehemiah 4:13-23

While trusting in God's provision and protection, Nehemiah was vigilant in preparing for the city's defense. Without a police force or a standing army, Jerusalem's security required citizen-soldiers. It's fascinating to observe this strategic leader. First, he stationed armed guards in "the lowest" and "open" places (Neh. 4:13).

Second, Nehemiah communicated what was at stake—the mission that God gave them and the families who counted on them. The remarkable Ukranian resistance to invasion demonstrates the power of such rhetoric. Notice the impact of his appeal: "we all returned to the wall, each to his work" (4:14-15).

Third, Nehemiah organized the workers to prepare for an assault by their enemies. He assigned half to serve as armed guards while the remainder continued to build. Even those moving stones "labored on the work with one hand and with the other held a weapon." (4:17).

Fourth, he set up a system to communicate if attacked. Since the workers were "spread out," a man with a trumpet remained at his side. Nehemiah instructed fellow leaders, "Rally to us wherever you hear the sound of the trumpet" (4:17-20).

Finally (and most important), Nehemiah continually reminded the population that they would not fight alone: "our God will fight for us," recalling how the Lord had delivered their ancestors from Egypt and kept the Philistines at bay (4:20).

Oliver Cromwell supposedly said, "Trust in God and keep your powder dry."[47] Nehemiah would have agreed. Somewhat whimsically, Philip Yancey wrote, "if Ezra was a saint, Nehemiah was a semi-saint."[48] The Persian cupbearer was not squeamish in preparing people for battle.

WRESTLING WITH ARMING

Avoid undue risk when on God's mission. Door locks, security systems, and common sense measures are no-brainers. Avoid unnecessarily dangerous situations. Nonetheless, we may find ourselves in risky situations. If so, we face a dilemma. While Nehemiah encouraged his people to take up weapons, Jesus Christ encouraged his disciples to seek creative alternatives to self-defense: "if someone strikes you on the right cheek, turn the other also" (Matthew 5:39). Those who follow Jesus are commended to "love your enemies and pray for those who persecute you" (Matthew 5:44). At the least, being disciples of Jesus requires us to wrestle prayerfully with ways we might respond nonviolently to physical threats.

If you conclude that taking up arms is a legitimate option, at least ask yourself, "Is this a situation so dangerous as to warrant the risks of carrying a gun?" Statistics tell us that a firearm is far more likely to be used against a family member, for a suicide, or be discharged in an accident than for self-defense. Furthermore, criminals usually "get the drop" on their victims. Raising a gun in defense may draw bullets in your direction. The reality is that in most contexts, arming yourself may increase the risk to yourself and your family members.[49]

There's also an increased burden on your emotional and spiritual health. The routines required to carry a firearm—loading, unloading, holstering, and securing—could be corrosive to your soul.

These risks might seem unnecessary when recognizing that most American Christians live and work in relatively safe communities. To be victimized by gun violence is statistically unlikely. The rate of violent crime has declined in recent decades: "Using the FBI numbers, the violent crime rate fell 48% between 1993 and 2017; using the Bureau of Justice Statistics data, the rate fell 74% during that span"[50] (This long-term decline has been interrupted by the disruptive impact of the COVID pandemic, hopefully this reversal will be temporary).

American Christians are unlikely to face physical threats. Yet because of around-the-clock news sensationalism ("if it bleeds, it leads"), the average American seems convinced that the rate of violent crime has been steadily increasing. *A paradox of our generation is that the perception of a growing threat persuades many people to take measures that inevitably raise their risk.* Anyone could justify arming themselves from anecdotal accounts of violence. Yet the reality is that in many situations, arming yourself for protection yields tragic consequences.

OUR OWN SAFETY

What if you enter a setting where the surroundings seem dangerous? Followers of Jesus don't allow fear to take over, for the Lord gives us his peace (John14:27). After Lynn and I announced our plans to move to a lower income community on the mainland, several men cornered me in the church lobby, "You ARE taking a gun, aren't you?"

My answer was "no." I explained that the risk wasn't high. Because of courageous neighbors, greater police vigilance, and the effectiveness of Neighbor Up Brevard and other community partners, the crime rate in our new neighborhood had dropped dramatically in the years prior to building our house. The remaining pockets of drug activity were several blocks away. We would settle for a home security system.

In the six years since, we've endured one unnerving episode. An exceedingly drunk fellow mistook our house for someone else's. At 1:30 am he yelled and banged on the front door, pulling on the locked knob. We called the police. Within five minutes he was cuffed on the yard.

I honestly believe that we're safer because we're not armed. If I were to draw a gun, an assailant would have the preemptive advantage. And while we have confidence in the police, we place our ultimate trust in our Almighty Father, who will vindicate us in Resurrection.

QUESTIONS TO PONDER:

1. In Nehemiah's context, why was arming workers for self-defense the right and faithful response to the threat posed by his enemies?
2. In your context, is arming yourself justified? While it is your constitutional right, in what circumstances should a Christ-follower arm himself or herself in response to threats or violence?

DAY 25

WHEN EVIL SEEKS TO DISTRACT

Evil powers are unrelenting in their opposition to God's benevolent purposes. To gain deeper awareness of how to overcome supernatural opposition, let's jump to Nehemiah 6:

> Now when it was reported to Sanballat and Tobiah and to Geshem the Arab and to the rest of our enemies that I had built the wall and that there was no gap left in it (though up to that time I had not set up the doors in the gates), Sanballat and Geshem sent to me, saying, "Come and let us meet together in one of the villages in the plain of Ono." But they intended to do me harm. So I sent messengers to them, saying, "I am doing a great work and I cannot come down. Why should the work stop while I leave it to come down to you?" They sent to me four times in this way, and I answered them in the same manner.   Nehemiah 6:1-4

The unimaginable was now reality—from piles of debris, sturdy walls had been rebuilt, and "not a gap was left in it." A discouraged and divided populace had been inspired, unified, organized, and sustained through six weeks of grueling labor. The effort to secure Jerusalem was nearly complete. All that remained was to set the massive doors in the city's gates.

Nehemiah's enemies had failed to halt the progress. Neither mocking the workers nor threatening physical harm had derailed the effort. The city would soon be a strong fortress. Just weeks remained for neighboring opponents to thwart this progress.

NEW LINE OF ATTACK

Sanballat and Geshem had nimbly pivoted from physical intimidation to subtle distraction. Instead of threatening annihilation, they signaled a desire for conciliation. Four times they invited Nehemiah to meet them on the plain of Ono, a seemingly safe location where they would ostensibly discuss terms for coexistence.

Such an invitation might seem to be a positive development. Walls and gates alone wouldn't guarantee Jerusalem's security. In the ancient world, armies would lay siege to cities, starving the population and eventually breaching the walls (as the Babylonians did to Jerusalem 140 years earlier). Nehemiah could easily have succumbed to this deceit.

Again, Nehemiah's prayerful discernment protected him from peril. He understood that "they intended to do me harm" (Neh. 6:2b). Even with armed escort, venturing from Jerusalem would put his safety at risk. His absence might alarm the residents. Without Nehemiah's presence, rivalries might spring up among subordinates. Without his vision casting, the workers' energy might falter. No, Nehemiah would not be distracted. Four times he replied, "I am doing a great work and I cannot come down. Why should the work stop while I leave it to come down to you?" (6:4).

PERILS OF DISTRACTION

Distraction is one of evil's most virulent weapons against hope-building. If mockery, fear of shortage, and physical threats seek to impede us, we readily recognize our need for divine intervention. *Distraction can be sinister because it's rarely recognized as Satan's tool.* Whatever distracts us may not be inherently evil. But if succumbing to distraction prevents us from keeping our attention focused on God's purposes, it does the devil's bidding.

Many Christians are ineffective in reaching their potential because they leave their TVs on and they waste hours on social media. (Full disclosure: I battle being a "news junkie" and have to resist the temptation to over-consume it.)

We live in the "age of distraction." Unless we emulate the Amish and get off the information grid, we must make an intentional effort to stay focused. Here's the good news: we're not on our own. Our Lord provides the remedy. Once we recognize the reality and name our vulnerability to a specific distraction, we can receive God's prevailing power. Quoting Proverbs 3:34, James reminds us that:

[God] gives greater grace. Therefore he says:

God resists the proud but gives grace to the humble.

Therefore, submit to God. Resist the devil, and he will flee from you. Draw near to God, and he will draw near to you.

James 4:6-7, CSB

Resistance to evil is sometimes called "spiritual warfare." By confessing your weakness and asking for God's power, you fight the forces that want to neutralize your impact. Until the resurrection completes us, overcoming distraction will require vigilance in setting and keeping boundaries. (For a "recovering news junkie," setting aside certain times to check the news allows me to give my full attention to what matters most.)

Beware also of opportunities that might seem God-given, but if pursued, they would get you off track. If it's difficult for you to finishing one project before starting another, you're susceptible to "purpose-drift." Casting vision and starting new projects can be far more exciting that remaining focused on the work to which God has already called you.

Well-meaning people can get you off track. After Jesus told his disciples about the necessity that he "suffer many things," Peter rebuked him (Mark 8:31). Jesus responded by rebuking Peter, saying, "Get behind me, Satan! You are not thinking about God's concerns but human concerns" (8:33). For leaders planting new churches, it's a continual battle not to drift from the clear vision that guides and energizes your fledgling congregation. It may be tempting to alter the vision or change the strategy when participants gush about their cousins' amazing congregation in Texas. Make course corrections only after a prayerful discernment process.

Sometimes those who seek to distract us have malicious intent. New projects are notorious for drawing participants who are emotionally and spiritually unhealthy. Often, they abandoned other organizations because they couldn't manipulate the leaders. Newcomers can seem "too good to be true" because they are. The health of hope-building projects depends on its leaders recognizing and resisting distractions.

Six years ago, the Lord infused Lynn and me with a vision to plant Church in the Wild, an intentionally missional congregation. Our aspiration is to involve Jesus-followers directly in God's mission to redeem and restore the lives of people who don't participate in a church. Rather than "go" to church, we strive to "be" the church wherever we are. Our goal is to help fellow disciples develop lifestyles that reflects the three-dimensional spirituality modeled by Jesus—a balance of worship, fellowship, and mission. When Jesus calls people to be his disciples, they worship God and benefit from deepening relationships as they participate in God's mission.[51]

To facilitate this goal, we chose to reduce the amount of time devoted to conventional worship services to twice a month. We've encouraged participants to use their "free Sundays" to worship God by living as missionaries—building relationships with "unchurched" and "de-churched" people through shared meals, service projects, backyard cookouts, and block parties.[52] As the Holy Spirit uses us to help neighbors become Christ-followers, we include them in micro-churches that meet in homes or public spaces on our "free weekends."

This ambitious vision requires our participants to win battles over distraction. If our participants go to other church services on the "free Sundays" or devote all the extra time to frivolous pursuits, they will have little time left for God's redemptive mission. Over the years, we've been disappointed to observe some of Jesus' disciples spent an inordinate amount of time on work, family, and hobbies. God's blessings can be idols if those blessings monopolize our attention. Of course, there are seasons of life when family needs or other responsibilities become our God-given priority. Far more common is the tendency for Christians to succumb to distraction from sustained hope-building simply because the demands of work, family, or leisure are insatiable.

Don't let distraction compromise your calling. There are times when we should tell the Tempter: "I am doing a great work and I cannot come down."

QUESTIONS TO PONDER:

1. Why might have Nehemiah been tempted to accept the invitation to meet his enemies on the Plain of Ono? What was the risk?
2. What tends to distract you from hope-building?
3. What steps can you take to overcome distraction?

DAY 26

WHEN EVIL STRIVES TO ENTRAP

Obvious attacks are the easiest to deflect. To this point, neither verbal abuse, sowing dissention, physical threats, treachery, nor distraction persuaded Jerusalem's leader to abandon his calling. The walls were finished. The gates would soon be hung. Sanballat's time was running out. In a last-ditch effort, he sought to entrap Nehemiah into making costly misjudgments.

In the same way Sanballat for the fifth time sent his servant to me with an open letter in his hand. In it was written, "It is reported among the nations—and Geshem also says it—that you and the Jews intend to rebel; that is why you are building the wall; and according to this report you wish to become their king. You have also set up prophets to proclaim in Jerusalem concerning you, 'There is a king in Judah!' And now it will be reported to the king according to these words. So come, therefore, and let us confer together." Then I sent to him, saying, "No such things as you say have been done; you are inventing them out of your own mind" —for they all wanted to frighten us, thinking, "Their hands will drop from the work, and it will not be done." But now, O God, strengthen my hands.

One day when I went into the house of Shemaiah son of Delaiah son of Mehetabel, who was confined to his house, he said, "Let us meet together in the house of God, within the temple, and let us close the doors of the temple, for they are coming to kill you; indeed, tonight they are coming to kill you." But I said, "Should a man like me run away? Would a man like me go into the temple to save his life? I will not go in!" Then I perceived and saw that God had not sent him at all, but he had pronounced the prophecy against me because Tobiah and Sanballat had hired him. He was hired for this purpose, to intimidate me and make me sin by acting in this way, and so they could give me a bad name, in order to taunt me. Remember Tobiah and Sanballat, O my God, according to these things that they did, and also the prophetess Noadiah and the rest of the prophets who wanted to make me afraid.   Nehemiah 6:5-14

By questioning his loyalty to the Persian king, Sanballat sought to panic Jerusalem's governor. Both men knew that Nehemiah's success could be perceived as a rebellion against Persia. Intoxicated with power, many leaders have an insatiable desire to promote themselves. Subordinates of Artaxerxes likely monitored Nehemiah's actions to ensure that the king's largess wasn't turned against him.

In contrast, the Lord desires leaders who subordinate their egos for the common good. The supreme example is David. He served King Saul faithfully, though David was better prepared to be king. Such leaders place their ambitions into God's hands. Leadership consultant Jim Collins calls these "Level 5 leaders"—those whose ambition for a cause is greater than their ambition for themselves.[53] Ensuring the security of Israel against the Philistines was David's driving ambition, so he submitted to King Saul. Establishing Jerusalem's defense against the Samaritans was Nehemiah's driving ambition, so he submitted to the Persian king.

Despite their good intentions, self-aware leaders recognize their potential to threaten others. It was unsettling for Nehemiah to hear rumors that he planned to make himself the king of Judah. Such lies would turn King Artaxerxes against him and Jerusalem's restoration.

Nehemiah kept his calm. His confidence was grounded in God instead of his own strength. Based on his previous pattern, likely he took time to pray, then emerged convinced that Sanballat was "inventing them out of [his] own mind" (Neh. 6:8b).

SANBALLAT'S LAST STAND

Nehemiah's enemies made their final attack—a clever attempt to trick the governor into self-destruction (6:9). A priest assumed to be Nehemiah's trusted ally became their secret weapon. Thinking that Shemaiah was "confined to his house" because he feared Sanballat, Nehemiah tried to encourage him. From this "friend," Nehemiah received a terrifying warning, that men "are coming to kill you; indeed, tonight they are coming to kill you." (6:10). Shemaiah urged Nehemiah to join him in taking sanctuary, "let us meet together in the house of God, within the temple, and let us close the doors of the temple" (6:10a).

According to the Law of Moses, Jews fleeing an avenger could take refuge at the altar outside of the Temple (Exodus 21:13-14). But entering the Temple itself was strictly forbidden by those who were not priests. Even King Uzziah had been afflicted with leprosy for burning incense in the Temple (2 Chronicles 26:16-21). As a priest, Shemaiah was allowed entrance to the holy place.

Nonetheless, Nehemiah knew that laypeople like himself were not allowed inside the Temple's inner court. Had Nehemiah not recognized this treachery, he would have lost God's favor and the people's support (6:13). Once more Nehemiah prevailed, because his trust in God gave him great awareness of his own heart and the hearts of people around him. As David wrote:

> For you are my rock and my fortress;
>   for the sake of your name guide me and lead me.
> Rescue me from the net that they concealed to trap me;
>   for you are my strength.   Psalm 31:3-4, ISV

Our gravest dangers are the traps set by Satan. Too often we are not aware of our vulnerability when evil manipulates our hearts or the people we trust.

CATASTROPHIC SNARES

In the wake of the personal catastrophe at the church I previously served,[54] I've sought to learn from my mistakes. One evening is painful to remember. I was eager to engage in conflict resolution with several staff colleagues but was told that face-to-face meetings had been delayed so the church's elders could interview former staff. It upset me to learn about secret meetings with anonymous accusers; these tactics seemed to contradict Jesus' exhortation that his disciples speak face to face about their concerns:

> "If another member of the church sins against you, go and point out
> the fault when the two of you are alone. If the member listens to you,
> you have regained that one. But if you are not listened to, take one or
> two others along with you, so that every word may be confirmed by
> the evidence of two or three witnesses.   Matthew 18:15-16

Jesus intended his church to be a prototype of peaceful conflict resolution, so my frustrations were valid. Encouraging anonymous complaints often yields biased and out-of-context allegations. Nonetheless, by losing verbal self-control, I stepped right into Satan's trap. By lecturing the elders with a raised voice, I reinforced the negative portrait crafted by my accusers. Had I been more spiritually aware and emotionally intelligent, my response would have been calmer, perhaps reassuring to elders shaken by allegations that I had bullied my staff.

I wasn't the only leader to step into a snare. My staff colleagues could have pursued conflict resolution, but they refused to communicate in a healthy manner. The elders and denominational officials could have insisted on face-to-face conversations, but unsubstantiated allegations against me seemed to infect them with bias. The spirit of Sanballat prevailed.

It's likely that reading Day 26 hasn't felt "inspirational." But if my saga makes you more wary of Satan's traps, recounting these painful stories is worthwhile. Peter instructs us to "Be clear-minded and alert. Your opponent, the Devil, is prowling around like a roaring lion, looking for someone to devour" (1 Peter 5:8, ISV). *Strive to be aware of your own brokenness and self-deception.*

Perhaps you will be openly confronted by people opposed to your hope-building. Yet the spirit of Sanballat is more often manifested through conflict that erupts within hope-building teams. Be prepared by practicing self-aware prayer. Nehemiah need not be the rare exception in avoiding catastrophe, for "greater is he that is in you, than he that is in the world (1 John 4:4, KJV).

Despite antagonism in the church, God's grace is at work. God continues to heal my heart and has restored me for pastoral leadership. Despite these ugly experiences, the Lord has infused me with a compelling vision for missional ministry. The Holy Spirit has reconciled several of us who'd been in conflict. Under new pastoral leadership, God is restoring the beautiful congregation that I was privileged to lead for twenty years.

Even our deepest lamentations can yield to God's praise:

> But this I call to mind,
>   and therefore I have hope:
> The steadfast love of the Lord never ceases,
>   his mercies never come to an end;
> they are new every morning;
>   great is your faithfulness.   Lamentations 3:21-23

QUESTIONS TO PONDER:

1. Why was Nehemiah more vulnerable to the temptation posed by Shemaiah than Sanballat's previous attempts to harm him?
2. As you read the author's painful account, do you recall a similar situation in your own life?
3. If you are involved in conflict, what steps can you take to pursue a peaceful resolution?

DAY 27

CELEBRATE AND PROTECT

Despite threats and distractions, Nehemiah's hope-building prevailed:

So the wall was finished on the twenty-fifth day of the month Elul, in fifty-two days. And when all our enemies heard of it, all the nations around us were afraid and fell greatly in their own esteem; for they perceived that this work had been accomplished with the help of our God. Moreover in those days the nobles of Judah sent many letters to Tobiah, and Tobiah's letters came to them. For many in Judah were bound by oath to him, because he was the son-in-law of Shecaniah son of Arah: and his son Jehohanan had married the daughter of Meshullam son of Berechiah. Also they spoke of his good deeds in my presence, and reported my words to him. And Tobiah sent letters to intimidate me.

Now when the wall had been built and I had set up the doors, and the gatekeepers, the singers, and the Levites had been appointed, I gave my brother Hanani charge over Jerusalem, along with Hananiah the commander of the citadel—for he was a faithful man and feared God more than many. And I said to them, "The gates of Jerusalem are not to be opened until the sun is hot; while the gatekeepers are still standing guard, let them shut and bar the doors. Appoint guards from among the inhabitants of Jerusalem, some at their watch posts, and others before their own houses."   Nehemiah 6:15-7:3

With singular leadership and countless sacrifices, the wall was finished and the gates had been hung—in fifty-two days. The people had secured their city. Their unparalleled success bore witness to the awesome power of the one true God. Nehemiah observed that "all the nations around us were afraid and fell greatly in their own esteem; for they perceived that this work had been accomplished with the help of our God." (Neh. 6:16).

Because of security concerns, the townspeople didn't celebrate the wall's completion till the gatekeepers and guards set safety protocols in place. Several weeks later, they gave God glory by reinstituting the Festival of Tabernacles, which we'll explore on Day 36. Their fifty-two-day work marathon would be chased with a party.

PAUSE TO PARTY

I once traveled to Haiti simply to throw a party. After years of partnership with CODEP (Comprehensive Development Project), our congregation was asked to subsidize a beachside celebration for several hundred Haitian *animateurs* (French Creole for "facilitators). The CODEP *animateurs* are grassroots leaders trained to equip their neighbors to reforest the barren mountains with fast-growing eucalyptus trees.[55]

After decades of sharing this hope-building vision, the fruit of the *animateurs'* labors was obvious. Driving west from Port-au-Prince, it's rare to see a large tree. Desperate people cut them for firewood—an ecological disaster. Denuded hillsides yield cataclysmic floods from modest rain showers. Yet as you continue west, forests begin to appear. After passing through Leogane, the hills become lush. Eucalyptus fragrance hangs in the air. Wherever CODEP's *animateurs* have influence, rainwater is absorbed by a verdant watershed, vegetables thrive in replenished topsoil, and selectively harvested trees yield precious cash.

Nearly a hundred of these *animateurs* traveled down the mountain for our all-day feast. Some waded into the ocean for the first time. The music and dancing were a blast, a memorable way to reward CODEP's *animateurs* and celebrate God's gift of hope-building.

Though Jerusalem was secure, Nehemiah would not relax until the best people and policies were in place. Though "enemies" had "lost their self-confidence," the opposition had not ended. Many Jewish nobles were intermarried into the family of Tobiah, the Ammonite (Jordanian) leader. His intimidation tactics continued as he manipulated family loyalties.

PROACTIVE PROTECTION

Instead of obsessing over Tobiah, Nehemiah's attention shifted: from building walls to building an organization. He appointed gatekeepers to keep the city secure. He selected musicians and Levites to sustain the community's worship. Inasmuch as Nehemiah had promised to return to Persia, he chose successors to take his place. Hanani—the brother who initially stirred Nehemiah's holy discontent with his candid assessment—would be mayor, for he continued to share Nehemiah's passion for city's welfare. To assist him, Nehemiah appointed Hananiah, the commander of the citadel who remained steadfast when attack seemed imminent. Nehemiah trusted both men because they trusted God.

Nehemiah also instituted common sense procedures. The gates would be shut before nightfall and remained closed till well past sunrise. Guards were assigned to strategic locations.

It is crucial to celebrate a team's accomplishments. Nonetheless, vigilance must be maintained. Seen and unseen enemies will continue to attack. We are wise to take steps to prevent the erosion or destruction of our community's accomplishments.

The key is to equip and deploy responsible people to sustain the momentum. Nehemiah reminds us that the primary qualifications for guardians of hope-building are 1) personal integrity and 2) trust in God. Mentoring and training men and women to fill such roles is never-ending necessity.

As Nehemiah instituted procedures to secure his city, your hope-building team would be wise to develop plans that preserve your progress. Shutting gates at night might seem obvious, but Nehemiah knew not to assume the obvious. Be explicit in naming how an attack on your work will be prevented or deflected. While practical procedures help to prevent physical attacks (lock the door, set the alarm), your greatest need is to prepare for spiritual assaults.

In the wake of the catastrophe that decimated my former congregation, I realized that I had neglected to teach key leaders the biblical principles for conflict resolution. I now strive to cultivate a culture of peacemaking. This section is a key part of my congregation's "Missional Disciple Aspirations" (See Appendix 1):

Knowing that missional partnerships will inevitably yield conflicts, I agree that:

+ When I am disappointed with others, I will gently share my concerns directly with them, seeking to honor Christ with forbearance, mutual understanding, and reconciliation.
+ If my concerns are not heeded, I will ask another Christian brother or sister to go with me as I attempt to speak the truth in love to the brother or sister who has offended me.
+ If I discern that the Holy Spirit is leading me to end my participation in Church in the Wild; I will communicate this decision to one of its leaders.

While these commitments might seem obvious, people are often oblivious to the obvious. *Preparing for conflict resolution is as wise as locking gates at night.*

When he negotiated a nuclear disarmament treaty, President Ronald Reagan was known to quote a Russian proverb: "Trust but verify."[56] As you enjoy hope-building success, make sure to *party and protect*.

QUESTIONS TO PONDER:

1. Does your hope-building team pause to celebrate successes? If not, how might you introduce celebration into your work rhythm?
2. Are you mentoring or apprenticing others for leadership? Who might you invite into such a relationship?
3. If you're not a leader, might this be a time to ask a leader to mentor you to take greater role in sustaining your community?
4. What preventative measures might your team institute to protect your hope-building project?

DAY 28

BATTLE READINESS

Evil is pervasive and powerful. How often have we witnessed these sad spectacles: church leaders self-destruct in moral failure...ministry teams suffer from low commitment...mission teams shatter over personality conflicts...neighborhood redevelopment succumbs to unrestrained ambition... justice advocacy falters in a climate of political polarization. Such heartbreaking outcomes aren't simply the fruit of human frailty or ignorance. There is more than meets the eye. To overcome opposition requires awareness and preparedness for spiritual warfare.

Christ-followers believe that Jesus' death and resurrection inflicted Satan with a fatal wound. Our triumphant Lord will return to finish him! In Revelation, John declares that the dragon's days are numbered. Evil will be destroyed when Jesus comes to redeem, refine, and recreate. A new earth will mirror heaven's harmony. Such enduring hope enables God's people to face present challenges with courageous joy.

In the meantime, we endure Satan's onslaught. Enraged with Jesus' victory, the mortally wounded dragon wages war on disciples who faithfully demonstrate God's reign. Nonetheless, we can defend ourselves with confidence. To "be strengthened by the Lord and by his vast strength," Paul reminds us to dress for success:

> Put on the full armor of God so that you can stand against the schemes of the devil. For our struggle is not against flesh and blood, but against the rulers, against the authorities, against the cosmic powers of this darkness, against evil, spiritual forces in the heavens.
>
> Ephesians 6:10-12, CSB

Our hope-building efforts will be far more effective as we heed Paul's warning: evil is personal, predatory, and powerful.

SPIRITUAL ENEMIES

The language of evil isn't a primitive way to talk about human ignorance or mental illness. Evil powers permeate our world. They are invisible yet real spiritual personalities unalterably opposed to God. The Bible provides a fleeting glimpse of a heavenly rebellion that introduced sustained sabotage into God's good creation.[57]

Since the Scientific Revolution and the Age of Enlightenment. Christians have struggled to "demythologize" superstitious medieval embellishments. Regrettably many theologians threw the proverbial "baby out with the bathwater," dismissing the biblical claim that evil has personal characteristics. While we do well to discard images of "horns" and "pitchfork," we fail understand our situation if we disregard the personal nature of evil. As C.S Lewis wrote:

> There are two equal and opposite errors into which our race can fall about the devils. One is to disbelieve in their existence. The other is to believe, and to feel an excessive and unhealthy interest in them. They themselves are equally pleased by both errors, and hail a materialist or magician with the same delight.[58]

Evil's personality is predatory. People's bad choices are goaded by delusional demonic powers. By describing evil as the "rulers...authorities,...cosmic powers...spiritual forces in the heavens" (Eph. 6:11, 12), Paul gives us a glimpse of the connection between rebellion against God in the spiritual realm and rebellion against goodness in our material world. Satan's minions are a bit like malware viruses created by computer hackers. Once introduced into software, these viruses have a life of their own. A malicious software virus "replicates itself by modifying other computer programs and inserting its own code."[59] Likewise, evil is the pervasive and aggressive disorder that we experience in an otherwise beautiful and benevolent existence. As with malware, Satan's viruses are programmed to replicate themselves and replace benevolent order with a self-destructive code. These viruses have aspects of intelligence and intentionality. They are aggressive, for "Your adversary the devil is prowling around like a roaring lion, looking for anyone he can devour" (1 Peter 5:8, CSB).

The analogy between a spiritual virus and a software virus resonates on a deeper level as we consider how the development of artificial intelligence will inevitably bring corresponding vulnerabilities. Artificial intelligence software enables robots to think and learn. Just as "dark powers" continually attack humans with spiritual malware such as lust, greed, hatred, and racism, robot designers will need to create mechanisms that alert machines to malicious viruses that could infect and incapacitate the robots.

You are continually besieged by spiritual malware that searches for your exploitable vulnerabilities. Don't make it easy for "cosmic powers of this darkness" (Eph. 6:12) by refusing to take them seriously. The disorder engendered by spiritual malware can do great harm and cause terrible suffering. This power is indirect. Satan harms people by tricking them to hurt themselves and others. In the 2016 election season, a foreign power magnified the hostility that many Americans felt towards fellow citizens by manipulating them with false social media personalities. Terrorists have been radicalized through jihadist or white supremacy websites. *Evil's power may be indirect and invisible, yet it is undeniable.*

The good news is that the devil has no more power than people grant, for "greater is He that is in you, than he that is in the world" (1 John 4:4, KJV). Unlike Jesus, Satan is not all-powerful. His power pales in comparison to God's power. As James promised, "Therefore, submit to God. Resist the devil, and he will flee from you"(4:7, CSB).

So why do we feel so vulnerable? Let's return to our comparison with software viruses. A solitary hacker may not have money, authority, influence or tangible weapons, but if he excels in writing malicious code and infecting vulnerable systems, he could bring down the electrical grid. Satan cannot make you sick, but he will tempt you to abuse your body. Satan cannot split a church, but the dark powers will continually strive to exploit its members' brokenness and narcissism.

PUT ON YOUR ARMOR

Since Satan is personal, predatory, and powerful, let's utilize the equipment that enable us to stand and fight with confidence:

For this reason, take up the whole armor of God so that you may be able to take a stand whenever evil comes. And when you have done everything you could, you will be able to stand firm.

Stand firm, therefore, having fastened the belt of truth around your waist, and having put on the breastplate of righteousness, and being firm-footed in the gospel of peace. In addition to having clothed yourselves with these things, having taken up the shield of faith, with which you will be able to put out all the flaming arrows of the evil one, also take the helmet of salvation and the sword of the Spirit, which is the word of God. Pray in the Spirit at all times with every kind of prayer and request. Likewise, be alert with your most diligent efforts and pray for all the saints. Pray also for me, so that, when I begin to speak, the right words will come to me. Then I will boldly make known the secret of the gospel, for whose sake I am an ambassador in chains, desiring to declare the gospel as boldly as I should.

Ephesians 6:13-20, ISV

Paul's imprisonment made him well-acquainted with military armor. Just as a Roman soldier wouldn't dare to report for duty in "scivvies," Christ-followers shouldn't face personal and missional battles without strapping on their gear.

+ **The belt of truth:** This piece of armor protects me when evil goes for my gut (figuratively speaking). To deflect a swordsman's jab, a Roman soldier wrapped himself with a thick, wide leather belt.[60] Aware of our vulnerability, each morning we should ask God to protect our emotions with the unyielding truth of God's provisional care. Whenever we are hit with bad news, God's truth will protect.

+ **The breastplate of righteousness:** The breastplate surrounds the heart with impenetrable bronze. The righteousness of Christ is bestowed in a great exchange: God replaces our guilt with the Savior's holiness. Even when we are unfaithful, God's righteousness isn't withdrawn. If we fail to remember God's faithfulness, the seat of our emotions becomes vulnerable to manipulation. As a soldier's breastplate repelled sword, arrows, and javelins, consciously claiming Christ's righteousness protects our inner being from Satan's attacks. We don't lose heart when remember that our righteousness is secure.

+ **Feet fitted with the readiness that comes from the gospel of peace:** The good news of Jesus keeps us going. Attempts to "be missional" without the gospel fail, just as no one could take a rocky path with bare feet. As a soldier strapped on shoes before marching long distances, "gospel shoes" keeps us on the path when hope-building is a marathon.

+ **The shield of faith, with which you can extinguish all the flaming arrows of the evil one:** Faith in God not only prevents Satan's accusations or manipulations from injuring us, it also thwarts his attempts to torch our accomplishments. Incendiary arrows stuck in the fire-resistant wooden shields burned out quickly. Soldiers kneeling in unison under raised shields were protected from a volley of arrows. Likewise, when hope-building Christ-followers raise their shields of faith together, they are invincible.

+ **Take the helmet of salvation:** By claiming our grace-given identity as God's children, we guard our minds from discouragement and deceit. Roman soldiers' helmets not only protected their skulls, the helmets covered their faces and their necks. When Satan co-opts other people to strike at our thoughts, we can be unshaken of our identity in Christ.

+ *The sword of the Spirit, which is the word of God:* Skill in wielding scripture makes us spiritual champions. After Roman soldiers put on armor, they took up offensive weapons. When Satan tempted Jesus for forty days in the wilderness, each lie was met with scripture, till the tempter left him. Memorizing key verses provides instant access to our spiritual arsenal.

+ *And pray in the Spirit on all occasions:* Communication with our High Command is the key to winning spiritual battles. By listening for the centurion's commands, Roman soldiers knew when to march in formation, to kneel and cover with shields, and to move forward on attack. Because Jesus prayed each morning, each day he went on offense. We are most dangerous to evil when we move in concert with our Commander.

John Wesley wrote that "no armor for the back is mentioned; we are always to face our enemies."[61] Though the prospect of doing battle with demonic power might be frightening, we fight with confidence, especially when we stand firm in concert with other believers.

Peter, Paul, and Nehemiah have shown us how to overcome opposition, even when it originates from the "cosmic powers of this darkness" (Eph. 6:10). Take these lessons to heart. Put on your spiritual armor each day. As Paul exhorted: "With this [awareness] in mind, be alert and always keep on praying for all the Lord's people" (6:18).

Before my catastrophe, I knew this passage well and was acquainted with "spiritual warfare." Yet I did not excel in wearing spiritual armor, nor did I sufficiently prepare my fellow-leaders for spiritual battle. In consequence, we were vulnerable. Our hope-building suffered horrible setbacks. Now I strive to remain alert. Consider yourself warned.

QUESTIONS TO PONDER:

1. Do you agree that evil is personal and predatory?
2. How is evil analogous to a malicious computer virus?
3. Which aspects of the "armor of God" do you sometimes neglect to wear?

WEEK 5

BUILD JUSTICE

Prior to completing the work of rebuilding Jerusalem's fortifications, Nehemiah's attention was drawn to a "great outcry" (Nehemiah 5:1). Natural disaster in the form of famine was aggravated by the influx of workers. If grain shortage were the sole issue, Nehemiah could have arranged for emergency food shipments and organized a distribution process. Yet this food scarcity was only the tip of the iceberg. The more intractable issue was the growing economic inequity due to predatory lending practices, land seizures, even enslavement. Such injustices violated the covenantal expectations that the Lord gave through Moses, which dishonored God and harmed God's people.

Nehemiah could have ignored the people's pleas. He might have shrugged his shoulders and said, "Sorry. Regulating business is not my concern." Sadly, turning a blind eye to injustice has been a common response by civic, business, and religious leaders. Yet upon hearing the cries of the oppressed, God cultivates prophetic leaders who recognize injustice and act upon their God-given discontent.

The Lord desires human communities to reflect His *shalom*, the Hebrew word for "peace with justice." Perhaps your own journey will provide the opportunity to honor God by building a better world. Jesus-followers agree with non-religious people that "every life has equal value," and that we should "work to help all people lead healthy, productive lives."[62]

Christianity is neither an escape nor a narcotic intended to distract or numb us to injustice. We are inspired and informed by the Exodus and the prophets. We are recruited and equipped by Jesus for the work of advancing God's reign. Therefore, we gladly partner with anyone who shares our commitment to social justice. In the process, we pray that our faithful witness will help our non-religious friends discover the joy of knowing their Creator, Redeemer, and Sustainer.

Let's fix our gaze upon the economic crisis Nehemiah faced while rebuilding Jerusalem's walls.

DAY 29

ATTENTIVE TO INJUSTICE

Hope-building work can stir up new challenges. Going back to Nehemiah Chapter 5, we discover that his Herculean rebuilding effort was threatened by dissention within the city:

> Now there was a great outcry of the people and of their wives against their Jewish kin. For there were those who said, "With our sons and our daughters, we are many; we must get grain, so that we may eat and stay alive." There were also those who said, "We are having to pledge our fields, our vineyards, and our houses in order to get grain during the famine." And there were those who said, "We are having to borrow money on our fields and vineyards to pay the king's tax. Now our flesh is the same as that of our kindred; our children are the same as their children; and yet we are forcing our sons and daughters to be slaves, and some of our daughters have been ravished; we are powerless, and our fields and vineyards now belong to others."
>
> I was very angry when I heard their outcry and these complaints.
> Nehemiah 5:1-6

When drought, pests, and disease bring shortage, the civic leaders' response makes a huge difference. Responsibility fell to Nehemiah, the governor of Judah. The needs were urgent. As Jerusalem's people declared, "we must get grain, so that we may eat and stay alive" (Neh. 5:2b).

The massive wall-building project worsened the famine's impact, bringing additional laborers into the city while depriving the countryside of agricultural workers. If it had been simply a famine-induced, construction-related shortage of grain, the situation could be remedied by importing and distributing grain. Nehemiah's administrative skills would hardly be stretched.

But this shortage wasn't only famine induced and construction related, it was magnified by a disastrous breakdown in the social fabric. The complaints were an appeal for justice, a "great outcry of the people and of their wives against their Jewish brothers" (5:1).

Specifically, land that didn't produce enough food had to be mortgaged to buy more food. This land was ultimately seized by lenders, leaving the landless poor unable to grow crops, with no alternative other than to sell their children as slaves (5:3-5). What a vicious, wicked cycle!

DEVALUING THE POOR

Injustice has often been dismissed as "God's will." Some religious systems legitimize an unjust *status quo*. Hinduism attributes injustice to *karma* and devalues a portion of the population, calling the lowest class of people "untouchable." While a cornerstone of Islam is the requirement to give alms to the poor, its adherents may respond fatalistically to injustice with the expression *in sha'Allah*, which means "God wills it." Despite the Bible's concern for social justice, unfaithful Jews and Christians have ignored or distorted its teaching to exploit others through slavery, colonization, and genocide. In the United States, Christians have sometimes opposed efforts to protect workers, provide an economic safety net, and guarantee fair treatment under the law.

Instead of responding with compassion, many people insist that poverty is a consequence of laziness and questionable character. The Bible most assuredly teaches that "If anyone isn't willing to work, he should not eat" (2 Thessalonians 3:10, CSB). Nonetheless, attributing poverty to individual irresponsibility is an insufficient explanation. I've observed many persons who are hard-working yet poor, eager for jobs that allow them to take responsibility for themselves.

A third way devalue the poor is to submit them to the whims of free-market capitalism. While unfettered capitalism often provides economic growth and prosperity that benefits some people, its "creative destruction" of inefficient, outmoded enterprises often marginalize workers, destroys communities, and harms the environment.[63] To advocate predatory capitalism without mitigating its impact on the poor is an attempt to remove God's concern for the poor from the public sphere.

GOD'S PASSION FOR JUSTICE

By contrast, scripture portrays God's tenacious concern for the poor. The Hebrew word for justice is *misphat*, which includes, but is not limited to, the quest for individual justice (signified by the blindfolded woman holding scales).[64] Yet *misphat* is a more holistic view of justice; it has a social dimension. *Misphat* reflects God's expectation that individuals also have access to economic opportunity. Biblical justice is concerned with whether God's people embody the covenantal principles expressed in scripture. Here are specific examples:

+ Property rights were not absolute; property owners were stewards of land on behalf of the community. For example, landless workers had the right to glean fields after the first harvest. The excess grain belonged to them, not to the landowner (Leviticus 19:9-10).

+ Financial capital could not be used to exploit workers. For example, no usury (interest) could be charged on loans to the needy members of the covenant community. Interest could only be charged to Gentiles (Exodus 22:25-27, Deuteronomy 23:20).

+ Wealth could not be accumulated by a small number of powerful families. For example, on the fiftieth year, called the "Year of Jubilee," land was returned to descendants of those who lost it through foreclosure in times of financial distress (Leviticus 25:8-10). At the end of seven years, financial debts were to be canceled (Deuteronomy 15:1).

+ Since poverty is inevitable in a world of birth defects, injuries, premature deaths, unequal capabilities, and unfavorable circumstances, the Israelites were commanded to be "open your hand" towards the needy (Deuteronomy 15:8, CSB).

+ God was expected to intervene to remedy injustice. When God's people disregarded the covenantal expectations, the Lord sent prophets to denounce specific offenses and demand repentance (Amos 2:6-7, 4:1-3, 5:11-13; Isaiah 5:8-10; Micah 2:2-5; Habakkuk 2:6-7).

Faithful to the scriptures, Nehemiah embraced these covenantal expectations despite his privileged position as the cupbearer to the Persian king. Knowing God's Word infused him with God's passion. He reported that "I was very angry when I heard their outcry and these complaints" (Neh. 5:6). As we will see, responding to their crisis complicated his work, cost him wealth, and made him enemies among the privileged class. *Yet by opposing injustice, Nehemiah added a vital dimension to hope-building.*

Humanity has benefitted from centuries of progress. In many places, the struggle for social justice has produced societies rich with educational and economic opportunities. Nonetheless, billions of people struggle with the challenges of daily life. Hundreds of millions are exploited by predators. More than 40 million people are enslaved as sex workers or laborers.[65] As Christ-followers, we strive to embody God's heart by helping people in disadvantaged situations.

INJUSTICE AMONG US

Even in the United States, we can see great disparity of opportunity, if we open our eyes. Years ago, I met weekly with a group of guys to drink beer, tell fishing stories, and debate current issues. Everyone but me lived in an affluent beachside community across the inter-coastal causeway. "As the crow flies," our neighborhoods were only three miles apart, yet my new setting was starkly different.

One night, the conversation drifted to our perceptions of the lower-income people living in "the hood." Several of my drinking buddies attributed their poverty to an "entitlement mentality." While not dismissing the possibility that an "entitlement mentality" affected some of my neighbors, I shared these observations:

> Guys, when my daughters turned sixteen, they both wanted to earn spending money. Despite the Great Recession, the oldest immediately got a job two blocks from our house at the new pizza place. Within six months, she moved to a health food sandwich shop. Likewise, my younger daughter was quickly hired at a nearby car wash. Soon afterwards she worked at a restaurant.

> My daughters were bright, hard-working teenagers. But two other factors were crucial to their getting those "first jobs." First, they lived near dozens of businesses needing entry-level workers. Second, they were the same race as the people doing the hiring, and they lived in the same beachside community.

> In my new neighborhood, I know dozens of African American teenagers with an ambition to work and earn income. Their earnings could help their families with bills, buy clothes, and pay for transportation. Yet most fast-food restaurants are far away. Few businesses in their area hire teenagers for that crucial "first job." Those who do the hiring are mostly white. Even if not prejudiced on account of race, many employers would be wary of hiring teenagers who live in a higher-crime neighborhood. Do they really have plenty of opportunities? Is it hard to understand why some of them make bad choices when offered easy money?

I usually keep such opinions to myself. That night, I had the courage to bear witness to injustice. My buddies seemed willing to be challenged.

Courage often emerges from passion. After getting to know hard-working teenagers who lack opportunities, my anger flared when they were presumed to have an "entitlement mentality." Since then, I've sought to employ teenagers from my new neighborhood for yardwork.

We can't fix all the world's problems. Nonetheless, as followers of Jesus we cannot avert our eyes or cover our ears, nor can we ignore the Lord's leading. Open your eyes and listen to the Lord's leading.

QUESTIONS TO PONDER:

1. What are ways to rationalize a lack of concern for the poor?
2. Describe two examples of *misphat*, the biblical concept of justice.
3. Which aspects of the Lord's covenantal expectations are new to you?
4. Have you observed injustice that kindles passion within you?

DAY 30

BREAKING SILENCE

It's commonly assumed that God's people are supposed to be "nice." Yet love sometimes requires us to act in ways that may not seem nice. It may not seem nice to get angry, yet anger was Nehemiah's loving response to the news that Judah's poor were exploited by economic predators. His right reaction was righteous indignation.

> I was very angry when I heard their outcry and these complaints. After thinking it over, I brought charges against the nobles and the officials; I said to them, "You are all taking interest from your own people." And I called a great assembly to deal with them, and said to them, "As far as we were able, we have bought back our Jewish kindred who had been sold to other nations; but now you are selling your own kin, who must then be bought back by us!" They were silent, and could not find a word to say.
>
> Nehemiah 5:6-8

Love does not allow righteous indignation to become unbridled rage. Nehemiah's initial response to the charges was "thinking it over" (Neh. 5:7). His thoughtful and prayerful manner was a huge leadership asset. Nehemiah acted decisively after considering alternatives and listening for God's direction.

It's always tough to decide whether to speak out. This dilemma presented itself prior to the completion of Jerusalem's walls, documented in Nehemiah 6:15 (Day 27). A savvy politician might conclude that with the walls unfinished, it wasn't a good time to stir controversy. It could be risky to confront Jerusalem's leading families while dependent on the resources they provided for construction. Also, Nehemiah probably wrestled with the reality that he was already in conflict with Sanballat, Tobiah, and Geshem. Would it be wise to make more enemies? Nehemiah could have promised the landless and enslaved poor that he would address their concerns at a more opportune time.

Nehemiah didn't wait. He emerged from "pondering" ready to confront the nobles who exploited their neighbors. Nor was he very nice about it. Nehemiah "accused the nobles and officials; [he] told them, 'You are all taking interest from your own people!'" By ancient standards, the interest rate charged wasn't exorbitant. The nobles had charged the people a "hundredth part" (Neh. 5:1, KJV), a rate of one percent a month. twelve percent on a yearly basis. In the Persian Empire, the interest rate was usually forty percent 40%.[66] Nonetheless, charging interest on loans to destitute Judeans was a direct violation of the Jewish Law. Peasant farmers already had difficulty raising the funds to pay back the loan principle—especially if their land had been seized.

The Lord's covenantal ideal was that every Jewish family would be free to work a parcel of land, knowing that the community would protect them from destitution:

> You may exact payment from a foreigner, but cancel whatever your brother owes you. Moreover, there will be no poor person among you, for the Lord will surely bless you in the land that he is about to give you to possess. Only be certain to obey the voice of the Lord your God. Carefully observe all of these commands that I'm commanding you today.   Deuteronomy 15:3-5, ISV

The beloved community that God intended for His chosen people had devolved into "survival of the fittest." Nehemiah recognized that his job wasn't only to rebuild city walls, but to restore the city's justice. He fulfilled God's expectation that rulers "defend the afflicted of the people and deliver the children of the poor, but crush the oppressor" (Psalm 72:4, ISV).

After confronting the city's leaders, Nehemiah called a "great assembly." He reminded everyone gathered that God's people previously "bought back our Jewish kindred who had been sold to other nations." Then he confronted them by naming their ludicrous practice of "selling your brothers, only for them to be sold back to us!" (Neh. 5:7-8a). This was a clear violation of Moses' Law: "If your brother with you becomes so poor that he sells himself to you, you are not to make him serve like a bond slave. Instead, he is to serve with you like a hired servant or a traveler who lives with you, until the year of jubilee" (Leviticus 25:39-40, ISV).

Surprised by this courageous candor, the nobles and officials "were silent, and could not find a word to say" (5:8). As we shall see, Nehemiah's willingness to speak up against injustice prompted the nobles to change their behavior. His boldness challenges us. As Martin Luther King, Jr. wrote, "We will have to repent in this generation not merely for the vitriolic words and actions of the bad people but for the appealing silence of the good people."[67]

BREAKING MY SILENCE

As our nation's civil discourse worsens, many shrill voices spouting extreme ideologies claim to speak for God. Instead of contributing to our quest for the common good, these angry voices unravel our social fabric and tarnish the church's witness. My personal policy has been to avoid potentially contentious political discussions with Christians who seem to lack intellectual honestly and emotional maturity. Nonetheless, in recent years the Lord has repeatedly compelled me to find my voice, "speaking the truth in love" (Ephesians 4:15). It has been especially important to address brethren who use social media to make toxic, unfounded allegations.

In one case, a participant in my congregation spent her time finding and posting "Alt-Right" smears and conspiracy theories. After the 2017 "Unite the Right Rally" in Charlottesville turned violent, she posted thirty-four racially insensitive allegations within four days, many with dubious veracity.

She and her husband had offered to host a missional gathering for our new congregation. I wrestled in prayer about the likelihood of losing them if I offended her. Yet how could we embody Jesus in our city if core leaders were disrespectful to opponents and reckless with truth?

After praying and consulting with other leaders, I made an appointment with the woman and her husband. As gently as possible, I shared my concerns about the tone and accuracy of her public persona. For three hours, we reviewed those thirty-four caustic Facebook posts. It didn't end well. She insisted that they were accurate and even declared that posting them was her God-given mission. They never returned to our fellowship.

Though the outcome was costly, I don't regret breaking my silence. I had hoped that she would heed my concerns. She and her husband could have kept fellowship with us. But at the least, our missional community was no longer compromised by someone with an ideological agenda that usurps Jesus' mission.

BREAKING YOUR SILENCE

Love sometimes compels followers of Jesus to speak the truth in a gentle, self-controlled manner. *Breaking your silence may not feel "nice," yet the Lord can use your courageous voice to refine the church, advance God's reign, and bless peoples' lives.*

QUESTIONS TO PONDER:

1. What's a social justice issue for which you feel passion?
2. Have you ever "not been nice" for Jesus' sake?
3. Is God leading you to break your silence in some manner?
4. What's your view of the author's decision to ask his parishioner to reconsider her Facebook posts?

DAY 31

RADICAL REMEDIES

Hope-builders admit their own complicity while naming ways to right wrongs:

> So I said, "The thing that you are doing is not good. Should you not walk in the fear of our God, to prevent the taunts of the nations our enemies? Moreover I and my brothers and my servants are lending them money and grain. Let us stop this taking of interest. Restore to them, this very day, their fields, their vineyards, their olive orchards, and their houses, and the interest on money, grain, wine, and oil that you have been exacting from them." Then they said, "We will restore everything and demand nothing more from them. We will do as you say." And I called the priests, and made them take an oath to do as they had promised. I also shook out the fold of my garment and said, "So may God shake out everyone from house and from property who does not perform this promise. Thus may they be shaken out and emptied." And all the assembly said, "Amen," and praised the Lord. And the people did as they had promised.   Nehemiah 5:9-13

Previously, we read that when Nehemiah broke his silence, he was met with silence. Jerusalem's nobles and officials could not deny that charging interest exploited the poor. He pressed his condemnation, declaring that their exploitation of the poor would disgust even the idol-worshipping Gentiles.

Then Nehemiah made a startling admission of his own complicity: "I and my brothers and my servants are lending them money and grain" (Neh. 5:10). He didn't specify whether his household charged interest. If so, the poor's "great outcry" prompted his own repentance. Either way, from that point on, Nehemiah leveraged his leadership for justice.

First, he insisted that the people should "stop this taking of interest," In effect, he restored Jerusalem's commitment to the Law of Moses. Then inspired by the Year of Jubilee—when debts were canceled and foreclosed properties returned—Nehemiah challenged the affluent to "Restore to them, this very day, their fields, their vineyards, their olive orchards, and their houses, and the interest ... (5:11).[68]

Amazingly, the crowd agreed. "We will restore everything and demand nothing more from them. We will do as you say" (5:12a). In response to inspired leadership, Judea's predators became fair-minded neighbors.

Ever the realist, Nehemiah insured that these mass conversions weren't short-lived decisions. Back in Jeremiah's time, the rich agreed to free their Hebrew slaves, but "afterward they turned around and took back the male and female slaves that they had set free, and they forced them to become male and female slaves (Jeremiah 34:11, ISV). Determined not to repeat this betrayal of God's covenant, Nehemiah summoned the Temple priests as witnesses and "made them take an oath to do as they had promised" (Neh. 5:12b). Utilizing prophetic symbolism, he shook out his robe to illustrate how God would "shake out everyone from house and from property who does not perform this promise (5:13).

To this, "the whole assembly said "Amen" and praised the Lord. And "they did what they promised!" Courageous leaders can influence others to repent of greed and act with generosity.

REPENTING OF AFFLUENZA

To fulfill his mission to restore God's reign, Jesus challenged his disciples to live simply, excel in giving, and repent of predatory commerce. With great love, he spoke inconvenient truths that transformed selfish exploiters into generous neighbors.

After recognizing the chief tax collector gawking from a tree branch, Jesus invited himself into the repugnant man's home. In return, Zaccheus invited his unsavory friends into Jesus' presence. Likely, Jesus spoke of his mission to restore God's righteous reign. Gracious and truthful presence are a powerful combination. Before dessert was served, Zacchaeus stood up and declared, "'Look, I'll give half of my possessions to the poor, Lord. And if I have extorted anything from anyone, I'll pay back four times as much'" (Luke 19:8, CSB). Don't you imagine that his accountant fainted!

Millard and Linda Fuller gave away a fortune. Theirs wasn't "ill-gotten gain." Millard became a millionaire through legitimate enterprises. Yet his obsessive entrepreneurship and idolization of wealth brought misery, nearly destroying the Fullers' marriage. At the brink of divorce, Millard and Linda opened their hearts to the transforming power to the gospel. In a cascading series of decisions, they sold their business, gave away the proceeds, and became resident partners of Koinonia Farm, a Christian commune in South Georgia. While living and working in Christian community, God infused them with the hope-building vision, called Habitat for Humanity.[69]

Lynn and I were inspired each time our paths crossed with the Fullers. In 1983, I joined Millard and three college students for a mile of his five-hundred-mile fundraising trek from South Georgia to Indianapolis. After Habitat became a household name, Lynn and I had the privilege of dining with Millard and Linda. Years later, they spoke to my congregation. Each time, I marveled at the Fullers' joy as they poured their lives into building partnerships for affordable housing. The radical remedy for their own "affluenza" has drawn millions of poor and affluent people into hope-building partnerships.

As with Nehemiah, the Fullers' radical self-remedy enabled them to ask much of others. In the early 2000s, our local affiliate brought Millard to Melbourne. Previously, the executive director sought a commitment from me to encourage my congregation's leaders to build three houses over an eighteen-month period. At the reception, Millard exclaimed, "Michael, how good to see you!" With a wink I declared, "Millard, after I left Atlanta, I suspected you'd track me down." The executive director interrupted our pleasantries: "Michael, before God and Millard Fuller, will you commit your church to build three houses?"

What could I say? Despite the sizeable commitment, I couldn't help but say, "Sure, I think we're up for it." I can't remember whether Millard shook out the fold of his garment.

Such is the compelling influence of hope-builders who give credible leadership to God's mission to the poor.

QUESTIONS TO PONDER:

1. What was the impact of Nehemiah's admission of his family's complicity in making questionable loans to the poor?
2. What gave Nehemiah the right to challenge the wealthy to cancel the debts of the poor?
3. In your opinion, what motivated the affluent to act with remarkable generosity?
4. For what purpose would you be willing to make a "big ask" of people with abundance?

DAY 32

LEAD BY EXAMPLE

Hope-builders strive for integrity, and history abounds with cautionary tales of idealistic reformers who became parasitic autocrats. This downward trajectory was memorably portrayed in the novel *All the King's Men*. After an elementary school constructed with inferior brick collapsed on its children, a courageous state senator in the rural South challenged the corrupt political establishment. Eventually, his populist charisma propelled him to the governorship. But his quest to "do good" transformed Willie Stark into a tyrant.[70]

Power often corrupts. How often growing churches, vibrant cities, and developing countries suffer from self-centered leadership. Nehemiah's legacy is a rare exception.

> Moreover from the time that I was appointed to be their governor in the land of Judah, from the twentieth year to the thirty-second year of King Artaxerxes, twelve years, neither I nor my brothers ate the food allowance of the governor. The former governors who were before me laid heavy burdens on the people, and took food and wine from them, besides forty shekels of silver. Even their servants lorded it over the people. But I did not do so, because of the fear of God. Indeed, I devoted myself to the work on this wall, and acquired no land; and all my servants were gathered there for the work. Moreover there were at my table one hundred fifty people, Jews and officials, besides those who came to us from the nations around us. Now that which was prepared for one day was one ox and six choice sheep; also fowls were prepared for me, and every ten days skins of wine in abundance; yet with all this I did not demand the food allowance of the governor, because of the heavy burden of labor on the people. Remember for my good, O my God, all that I have done for this people.
>
> Nehemiah 5:14-19

Nehemiah embodied the ideal public servant. During his twelve years as governor of Judea, he didn't abuse the lucrative perks at his disposal. Despite his predecessors' habit of taxing the population and consuming luxurious portions of food and wine, Nehemiah claimed that "I did not do so, because of the fear of God. Indeed, I devoted myself to the work on this wall" (Neh. 5:15b-16a). How leaders deal with financial matters reveals whether they submit their lives to God.

Neither did he nor his associates take possession of any land (5:16b). Indeed, despite the necessity of entertaining hundreds of officials, he "did not demand the food allowance of the governor, because of the heavy burden of labor on the people" (5:17-18b). Nehemiah was a servant leader. He anticipated Jesus' exhortation to his disciples, "So if I, your Lord and Teacher, have washed your feet, you must also wash one another's feet. I've set an example for you, so that you may do as I have done to you" (John 13:14-15, ISV).

LIVING ON LESS

We celebrated how Millard and Linda Fuller's magnified their influence by giving away their wealth. Rick and Kay Warren's choices followed a similar trajectory. In 2002 this megachurch pastor published *Purpose Driven Life*, which pioneered the forty day devotional format. Rick's book resonated powerfully with Jesus-followers and with those exploring faith. Within several years the book sold more than 20 million copies, making the Warrens rich. Unlike many celebrity pastors, they invested the overwhelming portion of their income in God's work. Three years later, Rick explained their choices:

First, we decided we would not change our lifestyle one bit no matter how much money came in. So I still live in the same house I've lived in for 15 years and I still drive the same Ford truck, have the same two suits, I don't have a guest home, I don't have a yacht, I don't own a beach house, we just said that we aren't going to use the money on ourselves...Second, I stopped taking a salary from the church... Third, I added up all the church had paid me over the past 25 years and gave it all back...And so now, we give away 90% and we live on 10%. [71]

Spiritual leaders who demonstrate such integrity have immense credibility. When serving as the pastor of a large congregation, Rick's example encouraged me to decline several cost-of-living increases and divert those funds to lower-paid staff. The influence of Bob Lupton and other Christian Community Development leaders was seminal in our family's decision to relocate our home to live in proximity to persons in poverty.[72] When God surprised us with a call to plant a mission-focused congregation, we were already prepared to live on less income. Several partners who joined us indicated that our choices influenced them.

Our lifestyle choices do affect others. Nonetheless, being an example to people isn't our ultimate motivation. Nehemiah was fully aware that despite his integrity and personal sacrifices, enemies would impugn his motives. *What matters most is the Audience of One.* While it may seem self-indulgent to point out his own sacrifices, Nehemiah was simply being transparent as he drafted his epitaph: "Remember for my good, O my God, all that I have done for this people" (Neh. 5:19).

QUESTIONS TO PONDER:

1. How did Nehemiah's refusal to enjoy the perks of his office affect the leaders who were challenged to "give back" properties they seized from the poor?
2. If you're a leader, are you willing to make personal sacrifices for the cause?
3. What signs would indicate that you're a workaholic? Do you show other signs of unhealthiness?

DAY 33

PARTICIPANTS MATTER

Hope-building often requires persuading potential participants.

The city was wide and large, but the people within it were few and no houses had been built.

Then my God put it into my mind to assemble the nobles and the officials and the people to be enrolled by genealogy. And I found the book of the genealogy of those who were the first to come back, and I found the following written in it:

These are the people of the province who came up out of the captivity of those exiles whom King Nebuchadnezzar of Babylon had carried into exile; they returned to Jerusalem and Judah, each to his town. They came with Zerubbabel, Jeshua, Nehemiah, Azariah, Raamiah, Nahamani, Mordecai, Bilshan, Mispereth, Bigvai, Nehum, Baanah. Nehemiah 7:4-7

The City of David was secured and restored, yet relatively empty. Adequate housing was in short supply. Because fortified cities were advantageous in the ancient world, Nehemiah may have assumed that the Jewish residents of Judea would flock to Jerusalem to rebuild houses after they rebuilt the walls. Yet people can be cautious. The Judeans couldn't be sure whether the city would be well-governed and able to withstand an enemy attack. Sociologist Everett Roger's "diffusion of innovations" theory estimates that only 13.5% of people tend to be "early adopters" of positive change.[73]

People's willingness to return or relocate into a community is a huge factor in its redevelopment.

Bob Lupton insists that the *presence* of invested individuals leads to greater, more significant change within the neighborhood—far more than *projects* or local initiatives.

...good neighbors are always preferable to good programs. Neighbors who are committed to the health of the community function much like a healthy body. Like white corpuscles in the bloodstream, neighbors rush to the invaded area to surround, neutralize and expel the infection-causing intruder. Their vigilance continues day and night, for they realize how quickly disease can be spread.[74]

Our hope-building efforts lose their luster if the intended beneficiaries don't show up. Have you ever endured these scenarios? You organize a "neighborhood watch" and few people sign up. Your missional community throws a block party, yet neighbors send excuses. Your ministry team starts a church youth program, but the teenagers have full schedules. Persuading people to participate is a necessary aspect of building hope.

MARKETING COMMUNITY

Convincing others to take advantage of an opportunity can be as challenging as creating it. To overcome their fears, it's beneficial if the intended participants:

1. Grasp the benefit of participation
2. Trust that it will be a positive experience
3. Expect to see familiar faces

Nehemiah wasn't just a wall-builder. He had a gift for settlement salesmanship, which he attributed to the Lord. His God-provided path was to rally the regional population. His first step was to "assemble the nobles and the officials and the people to be enrolled by genealogy" (Neh. 6:5). Chapter 8 will describe this assembly—the reading of the Law at the Water Gate (Day 36). Notification of the scattered population was aided by genealogical records (the list of clan leaders in verses 8 to 63).[75] This Water Gate assembly was cathartic for the Jews. We'll soon learn how Ezra's reading of the Law brought tears of repentance and shouts of celebration. The rebuilding of the Holy City was followed by the people's overwhelming desire to embrace of God's holy covenant, tangibly expressed in a "firm agreement" (9:38). Arrangements for daily Temple worship in Jerusalem were also finalized (10:28-39).

This dramatic revitalization of the city as a religious center magnified its attractiveness for resettlement. Chapter 11 chronicles how the leaders led, and how the people followed.

Now the leaders of the people lived in Jerusalem; and the rest of the people cast lots to bring one out of ten to live in the holy city Jerusalem, while nine-tenths remained in the other towns. And the people blessed all those who willingly offered to live in Jerusalem.

These are the leaders of the province who lived in Jerusalem; but in the towns of Judah all lived on their property in their towns: Israel, the priests, the Levites, the temple servants, and the descendants of Solomon's servants. And in Jerusalem lived some of the Judahites and of the Benjaminites.   Nehemiah 11:1-4a

The "Revival at Water Gate" spawned a wave of enthusiasm for Jerusalem, so the general population agreed to send a "tithe" of its people. One person out of every ten moved to Jerusalem. The city soon teemed with residents.

Our hope-building initiatives will require prayerful discernment about what it will take to draw people into community-blessing endeavors. When Lynn and I built our home at the junction of two neighborhoods, one African-American (Booker T. Washington) and the other primarily white (Sunwood), we sensed God's call to build bridges between our diverse neighbors. We began by sharing meals with individuals. In the process, we discovered that few residents of the white neighborhood knew anyone from the black neighborhood (and vice-versa). When our missional effort grew to seven people, we initially took the name "SunBook," to express our aspiration to involve people from both neighborhoods.

CONNECTING WITH NEIGHBORS

We suspected that simply inviting neighbors to a social engagement would be insufficient. Many people had lived in proximity for years, yet were strangers. Initiating "small talk" might be awkward, especially since they resided in very different communities. Unlike Nehemiah, we couldn't draw upon a common religious heritage.

We discerned that it would be wise to schedule gatherings on dates with civic significance. Our first backyard barbeque was on Memorial Day weekend. The invitations featured patriotic artwork. We announced our intention to honor veterans. This approach seemed to legitimize the gathering and boost the turnout. Before serving the food, we asked veterans to raise their hands and describe their service. We offered a prayer of thanks for their sacrifices, as well as for those who had died in service to our nation.

Four months later, our SunBook missional community hosted a larger "back-to-school" cookout. Seven months after that, our growing core of neighborhood partners organized a block party on the Saturday evening of Easter weekend. Our team hosted an egg hunt for several dozen children. Our church's worship band performed secular tunes in a driveway. About seventy neighbors enjoyed a beautiful evening. Before serving the chicken, I offered a prayer of thanks for Jesus' death and resurrection—a religious reference appropriate to the occasion.

After these early successes, the need to market our hope-building decreased over time. Many of our neighbors were eager to gather. Cookouts and block parties yielded joy-filled celebrations and authentic friendships among diverse people. Children regularly ask, "When's our next party?" In recent years our neighbors have joined us in putting on a children's Christmas pageant and a neighborhood-based Vacation Bible School. Now we call ourselves SoulFest.

Experiencing community tends to persuade reluctant consumers to become invested partners. In the early stages of hope-building, leaders do well to cultivate participation.

QUESTIONS TO PONDER:

1. Why would the rapid resettlement of Jerusalem be an essential step in fulfilling Nehemiah's vision for restoring the city? How did Nehemiah accelerate Jerusalem's resettlement?
2. Have you endured the disappointment of dealing with a poor response to your efforts to improve your church or community? What did you learn from the experience?
3. Which takeaways are helpful from "SunBook's" missional initiative?

DAY 34

CULTIVATE GENUINE FAITH

Authentic biblical faith improves our behavior.

But be doers of the word and not hearers only, deceiving yourselves.

If anyone thinks he is religious without controlling his tongue, his religion is useless and he deceives himself. Pure and undefiled religion before God the Father is this: to look after orphans and widows in their distress and to keep oneself unstained from the world.

James 1:22, 26-27, CSB

Concerned to see signs of shallow religiosity, James named two outward signs of our inward conversion to Jesus' lordship. First, each of Jesus' disciples should be personally engaged in providing practical assistance to vulnerable people: "look after orphans and widows in their distress" (Jas. 1:27b). Second, a Christ-follower pursues habits of personal holiness, striving to "keep oneself from being polluted by the world" (1:27b). Our salvation is holistic; it impacts every dimension of life.

These countercultural behaviors don't justify us before God. Rather, the grace of Jesus is what makes us righteous in God's eyes. This grace is transformative, receiving it cultivates religion that is "pure and faultless." (1:27b). God loves us where we are, yet takes us to where we ought to be.

We can resist positive change by making choices that "grieve God's Holy Spirit" (Ephesians 4:30, CSB). Sometimes we are conscious of these decisions. More often, we are unaware because we have been influenced by those who reduce the gospel to fit a particular ideology. Progressive Christians may focus on the Bible's concern for the poor yet disregard its teaching on human sexuality. Evangelicals often focus on sexual purity yet may neglect the Bible's concern for the poor. These selective views of biblical faith make it easier for politicians on the left and the right to weaponize distortions of Christianity for partisan purposes.

Even more distressing has been the growing popularity of the "Prosperity Gospel." When the gospel of Jesus Christ is reduced to a self-help message that echoes our culture's narcissistic obsession with personal fulfillment, concern for holiness and for the poor are both devalued.

Each of these forms of "Gospel reductionism" weakens the church's impact.[76] Liberal, conservative, and consumeristic distortions of Christianity each inoculate people against sustained hope-building efforts. Unless we allow God's Word to challenge our ideologies, religious faith becomes a thinly veiled expression of self-interest.

ANTIDOTE FOR "WORTHLESS RELIGION"

After challenging the church to aspire to "pure and faultless" religion, James offered this prophetic denunciation of favoritism, admonishing the disciples not to give "special attention" to the rich or "discriminate" against the poor:

> My brothers and sisters, do not show favoritism as you hold on to the faith in our glorious Lord Jesus Christ. For if someone comes into your meeting wearing a gold ring and dressed in fine clothes, and a poor person dressed in filthy clothes also comes in, if you look with favor on the one wearing the fine clothes and say, "Sit here in a good place," and yet you say to the poor person, "Stand over there," or "Sit here on the floor by my footstool," haven't you made distinctions among yourselves and become judges with evil thoughts?
>
> James 2:1-4, CSB

Jesus' disciples must treat everyone as an equally valued child of God. *Hope-building has an added benefit if we can help affluent, powerful people gain humility while poor, powerless people gain dignity.* Affluent persons need relationships with poor people so that they will have strong examples of faith, for "Didn't God choose the poor in this world to be rich in faith and heirs of the kingdom that he has promised to those who love him?" (James 2:5, CSB). The obvious answer is, "Yes, Christians who struggle with poverty are compelled to trust God, while those with abundance are tempted to trust in their wealth." This is a consistent biblical theme. The psalmist acknowledges God's compassion when people humble themselves and His displeasure with those who maintain their arrogance: "Indeed, you deliver the oppressed, but you bring down those who exalt themselves in their own eyes" (Psalm 18:27, ISV).

MUTUAL BENEFIT

Cultivate genuine faith by striving to connect diverse people in hope-building partnerships.

As Irene Summerford's influence soared in our community, she struggled financially. While she and Lynn raised hundreds of thousands of dollars to build the Dorcas Outreach Center for Kids (DOCK), she could not afford to keep her ancient car running. As she poured herself out for God, the Lord provided for her need. An affluent, retired couple became friends with Irene as they sat near each other in our congregation's weekly worship. This couple had provided resources for Irene's sidewalk Sunday School (called Project Light—a predecessor ministry to the DOCK). After praying over Irene's transportation challenge, they asked me, "Would it be possible to give Irene our car, and can we keep this gift confidential?"

"Of course," I replied. We arranged for them to deed the late model Toyota Avalon to the church, then I signed it over to Irene. Isn't it remarkable? Irene's friendship benefitted this couple by providing inspiration, and her neediness provided them an opportunity to give. Meanwhile their friendship affirmed Irene's dignity while their generosity enabled Irene to excel in her ministry.

HOPE-BUILDING DISCIPLINES

Jesus redeemed us so that we would embody his holiness. As Peter wrote, "But as the one who called you is holy, you also are to be holy in all your conduct" (1 Peter 1:15, CSB). God's transformative grace is the source of our righteousness. Fostering habits that position us to benefit from the Holy Spirit's presence will increase our yield of spiritual fruit (Galatians 5:22-23). As an athlete embraces rigor, Paul encouraged Timothy to "train yourself in godliness. For the training of the body has limited benefit, but godliness is beneficial in every way, since it holds promise for the present life and also for the life to come" (1 Timothy 4:7b-8). Disciplines that cultivate our hope-building capacity include:

- *Prayerful Discernment:* You can't provide attentive care to every needy person, so discern your missional focus. To give a whole-hearted "yes" to the opportunity to help anyone, you must say "no" to other needs. As you pray, ask the Holy Spirit to make you aware of the people and situations on which the Lord wants you to focus.

- *Life-Long Learning:* As the Spirit focuses your attention on other people's financial, emotional, relational, and spiritual needs, seek out mentors and educational resources that help you avoid dysfunctional and co-dependent relationships. Love of neighbors should foster dignity and self-reliance. Avoid "helping that hurts."[77]

- *Healthy Habits:* Proper nutrition and exercise will sustain your good works. Setting and keeping boundaries on media consumption boundaries will prevent distraction.

+ *Simplicity:* Reflect on your lifestyle. Do some of your possessions or pursuits demand excessive time and money? Do they limit your capacity to love neighbors and maintain personal holiness? Like suckers on the base of a tree, some aspects of our lives aren't evil. They don't threaten the "tree," but they divert the energy it needs to thrive. To bear more fruit, prune possessions and pursuits, so that more time and money are available for God's Kingdom.

+ *Accountability:* Seek relationships that challenge your assumptions; commit to meeting with a few trusted friends on a regular basis, that you might provide mutual encouragement and "motivate one another to love and good deeds" (Hebrews 10:24, ISV).

QUESTIONS TO PONDER:

1. As a Christ-follower, which gets more of your attention: love of neighbor or personal holiness?
2. How could addressing your weakness increase your hope-building capacity?
3. Did you become more aware of a hidden tendency to show favoritism as you read this devotional? How could you remedy the problem?

DAY 35

BIG IMPACT FROM SMALL GROUPS

Your greatest battle might be your struggle with expectations. Even as you learn to overcome opposition, calm dissension, revitalize burnouts, and deal with dropouts, you could face the reality that your efforts seem to affect only a few people. This realization can be discouraging. Trust that God's providential grace will magnify the impact.

After several years of cultivating a missional community in our home, the COVID-19 pandemic made it impossible to share meals. Other missional initiatives screeched to a halt. Our church's core group shrank as participants gave up hope that our nascent congregation would ever take root. When we restarted socially distant, in-person gatherings, a portion of the remnant could only join us via Zoom or livestream.

Church leaders everywhere struggled with despair during the pandemic. We clung tenaciously to Paul's exhortation: "Let us not get tired of doing good, for we will reap at the proper time if we don't give up" (Galatians 6:9, CSB). Despite the social distancing necessitated by COVID, we found silver linings in the gloom. Our preference for micro-church gatherings became advantageous. While block parties and BBQs went on hold, the small size of our discipleship gatherings (three to five participants) and house churches (twelve to twenty participants) allowed these five micro-church expressions to meet at outdoor restaurants, beer gardens, porches, or back yards.

The Lord promised his initial band of believers that despite their small size, they would have huge impact. Jesus declared, "You are the salt of the earth" (Matthew 5:13). Distinctiveness is the key. Sprinkling a little salt makes bland food palatable. Rubbing salt into meat preserves it from decay. When Christ-followers embody his grace and truth, our presence preserves humanity and give life flavor.

Jesus also described his disciples as "the light of the world" (5:14). We are not the light. Jesus is the Light (John 9:5). As is illustrated beautifully at a Christmas Eve candle lighting service, those who bear the life of Jesus beautifully reflect his light, despite their flaws.

A small measure of light has remarkable impact. A single candle illuminates a room. Moonlight makes a dark path visible. Likewise, seemingly ordinary people brighten the world around them as they bear the light of Christ.

This positive impact is magnified in community, for "a city on a hill cannot be hidden" (Matthew 5:14b). Jesus underscored this point by using the second person plural form of "you." Matthew's Greek verbiage is literally: "You all are the light of the world." A Southern rendition would be "Y'all are the light of the world… or for emphasis: "All y'all…are the light of the world!" Genuine Christian community functions as a "colony of heaven on earth."[78]

After retiring to Britain, Dr. Leslie Newbigin was stunned to discover that the Christian community that sent him to India forty years prior had shrunk dramatically. Drawing on his experience as a missionary, Newbigin's writings heralded the need for a missional awakening. He encouraged congregations to become gospel-centered communities of care. Simply by striving to embody Jesus' counter-cultural ethos, Christ-followers would provide "plausibility structures" that gave credibility to Jesus' message.[79] Even small churches, if focused on embodying God's reign in Jesus Christ, can be "a city built on a hill [which] cannot be hid" (Matthew 5:14). A congregation declining in size can still have remarkable influence if its members' desire to embody the gospel surpasses their yearning to preserve the church as they've known it. In our increasingly post-Christian culture, the swelling ranks of skeptics need to glimpse the "real deal."

RELATIONAL IMPACT

Christian community is most authentic when it's small. A shared commitment to fulfill these New Testament's "one another" passages demonstrates the advent of God's reign:

+ Accept one another (Romans 15:7)
+ Be kind and compassionate to one another (Ephesians 4:32)
+ Offer hospitality to one another (1 Peter 4:9)
+ Be patient with one another (Ephesians 4:2)
+ Serve one another in love (Galatians 5:13)
+ Carry each other's burdens (Galatians 6:2)
+ Confess your sins to each other (James 5:16)
+ Pray for each other (James 5:16)
+ Forgive each other (Ephesians 4:32)
+ Live in harmony with one another (Romans 12:16)
+ Bear with one another (Colossians 3:13)
+ Submit to one another (Ephesians 5:21)
+ Be devoted to one another (Romans 12:10)
+ Encourage each other (1 Thessalonians 5:11)
+ Build each other up (1 Thessalonians 5:11)
+ Teach one another (Colossians 3:16)

+ Admonish one another (Colossians 3:16)
+ Spur each other on to love and good deeds (Hebrews 10:24)

Each of these admonitions is a specific aspect of what it means to "love one another" (John 13:34). Smallness is the key. Bible studies and life groups can be a genuine experience of Christian community—if "one anothers" are practiced. Hope-building groups provide the best environment, for "one anothers" are most applicable when disciples bless the world together.

IMPACT ON THE WORLD

Even institutional forms of Christian community that struggle with numerical decline can have amazing influence. The only factory in a rural county was shuttered due to overseas outsourcing. The economic impact was devastating. Collapsing tax revenues forced the school board to impose major budget cuts. The elementary school's arts program was eliminated.

Even before the factory closure, a tiny congregation in the town could barely afford a full-time, seminary-trained pastor. After the closure, the church lost more members. No longer could it raise sufficient funds to pay the pastor. Its leaders contemplated dissolving the congregation.

Amidst this gloom, a ray of hope emerged. Years prior, a member of the congregation had been mentored by a seminary-trained pastor to be a lay pastor. Fellow church members affirmed his leadership gifts. As church leaders faced their inability to afford a full-time pastor with seminary training, a revolutionary idea swept through the meeting. Why not invite the layman to be their pastor? He could shepherd the flock on a part-time basis. A modest stipend would supplement the income from his secular job.

This solution not only provided worship leadership and pastoral care, it also allowed the congregation to cultivate a stronger missional presence. The reduced cost of the new leadership yielded a budget surplus. In a second Spirit-led move, the church's elders hired the unemployed elementary arts teacher on a part-time basis to teach an after-school arts program in the church's basement. The aging congregation hosted dozens of elementary-age children and their parents. Bible stories were shared alongside art lessons. Families with children found their way to Sunday worship.

Since God is relational, *His Kingdom is most visible in small groups that prioritize relationships.*

When your labors seem insignificant, remember that our faithfulness in cultivating Christian community provides salt for the earth and light for the world. As William Watkinson declared, "It is better to light the candle than to curse the darkness."[80]

QUESTIONS TO PONDER:

1. What is the significance of Jesus using the *plural* form of "you" when he said that "You are the light of the world"?
2. Which of the "one anothers" have your experienced in Christian community?
3. Which "one anothers" have you not yet experienced?
4. How has this devotional encouraged you?

WEEK 6

CULTIVATE
TRUE WORSHIP

Completing Jerusalem's wall-restoration commenced a season of cele-bratory worship. Sensing the Lord's powerful presence through their city's transformation, the Jewish people gathered to give God praise and hear God's Word. It's likely that few of them anticipated how rebuilding the city would cultivate the restoration of their hearts.

REFRESHMENT AT THE WATER GATE

Hope-building fosters true worship:

Seven months later, the Israelis had settled in their own cities. All the people gathered as a united body into the plaza in front of the Water Gate. They asked Ezra the scribe to bring out the Book of the Law of Moses, which the Lord had commanded for Israel. So on the first day of the seventh month, Ezra the priest brought out the Law before the assembled people. Both men and women were in attendance, as well as all who could understand what they were hearing.

Ezra read from it, facing the plaza in front of the Water Gate, from early in the morning until mid-day in the presence of the men and women, as well as all who could understand. All the people were attentive to the Book of the Law. Ezra the scribe stood on a wooden rostrum erected for that purpose. Beside him to his right stood Mattithiah, Shema, Anaiah, Uriah, Hilkiah, and Maasseiah. Beside him to his left stood Pedaiah, Mishael, Malchijah, Hashum, Hashbaddanah, Zechariah, and Meshullam.

Ezra opened the book in the sight of all the people. Because he was visible above all the people there, as he opened it, all the people stood up. Ezra blessed the Lord, the great God, and with uplifted hands, all the people responded, "Amen! Amen!" They bowed down and worshipped the Lord prostrate on the ground.

Furthermore, Jeshua, Bani, Sherebiah, Jamin, Akkub, Shabbethai, Hodiah, Maaseiah, Kelita, Azariah, Jozabad, Hanan, Pelaiah, and the descendants of Levi taught the Law to the people while the people remained standing. They read from the Book of the Law of God, distinctly communicating its meaning, so they could understand the reading.   Nehemiah 7:73b-8:1-8, ISV

As a teenager, I was interested both in the Bible and current events. Imagine my fascination when a man I admired declared that a current controversy was prophesied in scripture. After reading Nehemiah's reference to the "Water Gate," he denounced the Watergate Investigation as "Satan taking down a good president." Suddenly, my thirteen-year-old-self sensed the possibility of taking scripture out of context.

Nehemiah's Water Gate had nothing to do with Nixon's troubles. From Nehemiah 3:26 we know that the Water Gate was the Temple's closest entrance to the Gihon Spring, Jerusalem's primary source of fresh drinking water. This gate opened to a spacious town square that hosted the climactic event of Jerusalem's restoration, when Ezra the High Priest read from the Torah—the Jews' formative scriptures.

The symbolism was obvious: God's people gathered to drink from God's Word, a vital source of spiritual life. The timing was intriguing. The first day of the seventh month (October 8, 445 B.C.) was New Year's Day on the Jewish calendar, the Feast of Trumpets (Rosh Hashanah, prescribed in Leviticus 23:23-25)[81]. Standing in their restored city, Jerusalem's residents were spiritually renewed as they entered a new year.

Ezra had returned from exile carrying a copy of the Torah thirteen years previous (Ezra 7:14). The Temple had been rebuilt by an earlier wave of returnees. Religiously mixed marriages weakened the pioneers' commitment to the one true God, so Ezra challenged them to build households devoted to the Lord. His influenced peaked as the city was restored.

The culmination of Nehemiah's work wasn't completing the construction. The pinnacle of his success was providing Ezra a platform (literally and figuratively) to teach the city's residents to build their households on God's Word. Because of Nehemiah, Ezra "stood on a wooden rostrum" while men, women, and children stood from daybreak to noon to hear Ezra read from the Pentateuch—the first five books of our Old Testament (Neh. 8:2-4, ISV). Having participated in a wall-raising miracle, God's people hungered to learn of the mighty acts that fashioned their ancestors into a covenant people. As Ezra read, "all the people listened attentively" (8:3). As he "blessed the Lord… with uplifted hands, all the people responded, 'Amen! Amen!' They bowed down and worshipped the Lord prostrate on the ground" (8:6). Participating in God's work cultivated their reverence for God's Word.

We bless people when we foster their desire to "listen attentively" to God's Word (8:3).

HELPING PEOPLE HEAR GOD

Notice Ezra's and the Levites' readiness to deal with a practical obstacle to the people's receptivity. Unfamiliarity with the Torah would confuse the listeners. Jerusalem's residents might not have been fluent in Hebrew, so Ezra's assistants translated God's Word into Aramaic.[82] After Ezra finished a section, we are told that the Levites instructed the people in the Law while the people were standing there "...distinctly communicating its meaning, so they could understand the reading" (8:7-8). Spiritual food was offered in bite-sized explanations.

There's no denying the rise of biblical illiteracy in our culture. Building hope increases our opportunities for disciple-making. Christians who've had a poor diet of God's Word often develop a hearty appetite as they engage in God's mission. Non-believers can be more receptive to Bible study after hope-building experiences opens their minds and softens their hearts.

So how will we respond? Do we dare to "feed" people who get pangs of spiritual hunger while on God's mission?

GETTING SMALL TO GO DEEP

The leaders of the conventional church that I served for several decades took great satisfaction in the high percentage of members who participated in Christian education. Two-thirds of the congregation shared fellowship and Bible study in one of fifty-five Life Groups. We also offered in-depth courses on Bible, theology, and church history. On a programmatic level, the results were remarkable. Many of the church's new members developed significant friendships and enjoyed mutual caregiving. Many new-to-faith people learned the basics of Christian discipleship. Of course, the congregation benefitted from this high level of involvement.

Sadly, this programmatic success didn't necessarily cultivate deep spiritual transformation. Over time, it became apparent that neither Life Groups nor classes were effective in helping participants address or overcome deeply rooted sin or brokenness. Self-destructive compulsions and addictions seemed immune to programmatic prescriptions.

Furthermore, virtually no one who had participated in our Life Groups or classes became "reproducible" (able to able to make disciples). We had cultivated their dependency on clergy or other trained leaders instead of preparing them to be disciple-makers themselves.

It's become apparent that the remedy for this disciple-making mediocrity is to encourage men and women to participate in small "accountability groups" composed of two to four participants of the same gender. Smaller group size creates a realistic setting for people have the time to talk openly and build trust. Smallness provides flexibility when meetings must be rescheduled, so participation is maximized.

Many resources are available to hope-builders who aspire to foster disciple-making. Discover Bible Study (DBS) is an international movement that promotes informal, lay-led discussions of scripture so that participants can provide mutual support as they strive to follow Jesus. Because of its remarkable simplicity, DBS is reproducible. Participants are soon prepared to start their own groups in homes, offices, coffee shops, and breweries.[83]

A more content-driven approach is to form "triads" of three to four people for rigorous study of a scripture-based discipleship workbook. Instead of depending on a teacher, participants invest several hours in preparation. After finishing six to twelve months of preparation, each triad member is equipped to lead a triad himself or herself.[84]

In addition to being personally transformative, micro-group discipleship inspires and equips participants to make disciples themselves. Disciple reproducibility was the main reason why Christianity spread rapidly in the ancient world. As Paul reminded Timothy, the young man he had mentored: "what you have heard from me through many witnesses entrust to faithful people who will be able to teach others as well" (2 Timothy 2:2, CSB). Paul taught Timothy is such a manner that he learned how to teach others who could teach others.

Get small to go deep. Ask the Lord to help you envision how you might find or start a three to four person discipleship group. Who of your hope-building partners might be willing to join you in a deepening spiritual journey?

The most profound hope-building isn't restoring a neighborhood or helping people succeed. Our ultimate goal is to help human beings know their Creator, Redeemer, and Sustainer…and give God glory. All other accomplishments only last a season. Human beings can last forever!

Let's build what lasts.

QUESTIONS TO PONDER:

1. How did Ezra's and Nehemiah's work come together at the Water Gate?
2. Why were God's people receptive to God's Word?
3. Can you envision yourself in an small "accountability group"?
4. What personal barriers keep you from being a reproducible disciple?

DAY 37

RELISH GRACE

Feasting upon the Word of God can be transformative.

Because all the people were weeping as they listened to the words of the Law, Nehemiah the governor, Ezra the priest and scribe, and the descendants of Levi who taught the people told everyone, "This day is holy to the Lord your God. Do not mourn or weep." He also told them, "Go eat the best food, drink the best wine, and give something to those who have nothing, since this day is holy to our Lord. Don't be sorrowful, because the joy of the Lord is your strength."

The descendants of Levi also calmed all the people by saying, "Be still, for the day is holy. Don't be sorrowful!"

So all the people went to eat, to drink, to send something to those who had nothing, and to celebrate with great joy, because they understood the words that were being declared to them.

Nehemiah 8:9-12, ISV

The Water Gate worship began with joyous praise. Yet feeding upon God's Word gave the people "spiritual heartburn," for "all the people were weeping as they listened to the words of the Law" (Neh. 8:9b, ISV). Rediscovering the Lord's covenantal expectations exposed their unfaithfulness.

We should grieve over sin whenever we discover that we've rebelled against God and harmed people. How tragic that contemporary culture often discourages people from taking responsibility for their bad choices. The popular show "Seinfeld" captured the *zeitgeist* of our age whenever Jerry, Elaine, George, or Kramer declared: "Not that there's anything wrong with that."

On the contrary, to restore wholeness, we must grieve over our brokenness. The good news of God's grace is meaningless unless we face the bad news that we have dishonored God and damaged people. As the beloved apostle wrote, "If we confess our sins, [God] is faithful and righteous to forgive our sins and to cleanse us from all unrighteousness" (1 John 1:9, CSB). The Bible consistently recommends honesty, repentance, and restoration for personal wholeness and for the health of the community. In the contemporary recovery movement, we see recognition of this need. No less than seven of the "Twelve Steps" of recovery focus on personal confession and reconciliation.[85]

After imagining Henry Ward Beecher's thoughts when he faced public disgrace, Frederick Buechner mused about what the 19th-century preacher saw when he cut himself shaving:

> The Gospel is bad news before it is good news. It is the news that man is a sinner, to use the old word, that he is evil in the imagination of his heart, that when he looks in the mirror all in a lather what he sees is at least eight parts chicken, phony, slob. That is the tragedy. But it is also the news that he is loved anyway, cherished, forgiven, bleeding to be sure, but also bled for. That is comedy.[86]

IRREPRESSIBLE JOY

God delights in pouring out grace upon those who own their sin. Jerusalem's leaders interrupted the wailing to assure the people: "'This day is holy to the Lord your God. Do not mourn or weep'" (Neh. 8:9, ISV). Rather than allowing the people to wallow in guilt, Nehemiah encouraged them to relish the tangible symbols of God's generous provision: "Go eat the best food, drink the best wine, and give something to those who have nothing, since this day is holy to our Lord" (8:10a). Years later, Jesus reaffirmed the good news of Water Gate: "Blessed are those who mourn, for they will be comforted" (Matthew 5:4, CSB).

To punctuate this great news, Nehemiah declared "'Don't be sorrowful, because the joy of the Lord is your strength.'" (8:10b). This simple phrase jumps of the page as Nehemiah's foundational conviction; indeed, feasting upon the Lord's joy transformed his holy discontent into sustained hope-building.

The joy of the Lord can be your source of strength, for the medley of joy reverberates God's grace. In the original New Testament documents, the two words are irrevocably connected. In Koine Greek, the word for "joy" is *kara*, and the word for "grace" is *karis*. God's grace (*karis*) yields human joy (*kara*). Divine joy welling us within us fuels gracious hope-building.

Fear, guilt, or necessity may prompt hope-build activity, yet on our own, we lack sufficient stamina to sustain good works. Our indefatigable source of strength is God's overflow of grace.

REMEMBERING OUR GRACIOUS PROVIDER

After their Water Gate catharsis, Jerusalem's Jews reclaimed an annual festival that grounded them in collective memories of God's sustaining grace. After reading the twenty-third chapter of Leviticus, they reinstituted the Festival of Booths, so like their ancestors, they "may know that I made the people of Israel live in booths when I brought them out of the land of Egypt: I am the Lord your God" (Lev. 23:44):

The next day, the heads of the families of all the people were gathered together, along with the priests and the descendants of Levi, to meet with Ezra the scribe in order to understand the words of the Law. They found written in the Law that the Lord had commanded through Moses that the Israelis were to live in tents during the festival scheduled for the seventh month. So they circulated a proclamation throughout their towns and in Jerusalem. It said, "Go out to the hill country and bring back olive branches, wild olive branches, myrtle branches, palm branches, and branches of mature trees, in order to set up tents, as has been written."

Then the people went out and found branches to make tents for themselves on the roofs of their houses, in their courtyards, and in the courts of God's Temple, in the plaza near the Water Gate, and in the plaza near the Gate of Ephraim. The entire assembly of those who had returned from exile erected tents and lived in them. Indeed, from the days of Nun's son Joshua until that day the Israelis had not done so. Joy was everywhere, and Ezra continued to read from the Book of the Law of God day by day, from the first day through the last. They celebrated for seven days, and on the eighth day they held a solemn assembly according to regulation. Nehemiah 8:13-18, ISV

Restoring the annual tradition of camping in leafy shelters was a powerful way to remind adults and teach children to trust God for provision and protection. The newly freed slaves had been vulnerable in the desert, yet God protected them. They lived with the constant fear of starvation, yet God provided manna. Remembering this legacy of abundance was pivotal for God's people. Maintaining their identity provided the key to claiming God's promise that "through you all the people of the earth will be blessed" (Genesis 12:3b, ISV).

Church camping trips don't begin to give Gentile Christians a taste of what Festival of Booths means for Jews. We would do well to fashion rituals that help us remember our experience of being stretched as we took steps to restore a neighborhood, plant a church, pioneer a ministry, or revive a dying congregation. Even when we feel that we are wandering aimlessly through the wilderness, we should remember that God has always sustained us through His providential presence.

The most significant "ritual of remembering" has been handed down to us. Sharing Holy Communion reminds us of Jesus' sacrifice, the epicenter of God's grace. Celebrating the Lord's Supper helps us remember God's greatest provision.

QUESTIONS TO PONDER:

1. What caused Jerusalem's Jews to weep?
2. What is the positive impact of confessing sin?
3. When are you most likely to experience the overflow of God's joy?
4. What creative rituals help you remember God's grace and provision in your hope-building journey?

DAY 38

DEEP CONFESSION

Hope-building can lead to soul-searching.

Nehemiah's quest to improve civic life catalyzed the people's spirituality. Having experienced God at work among them and within them, the Jews listened to Ezra's reading of the Law with open minds and broken hearts. As the writer of Hebrews testifies, "For the word of God is living and active, sharper than any double-edged sword, piercing until it divides soul and spirit, joints and marrow, as it judges the thoughts and purposes of the heart" (4:12, ISV). With fresh awareness of their guilt, the Israelites feasted upon God's grace. As Chapter 9 begins, it's obvious that God's people knew their need for life change:

> Now on the twenty-fourth day of this month the people of Israel were assembled with fasting and in sackcloth, and with earth on their heads. Then those of Israelite descent separated themselves from all foreigners, and stood and confessed their sins and the iniquities of their ancestors. They stood up in their place and read from the book of the law of the Lord their God for a fourth part of the day, and for another fourth they made confession and worshiped the Lord their God.
> Nehemiah 9:1-3

Public self-abasement was a feature of repentance for ancient Jews. In the wake of Jesus' redemptive grace, few Christians fast, wear sackcloth, or mark themselves with ashes when repenting of sin (other than Ash Wednesday). More common in our context is personal disclosure to a counselor, accountability partners, or a recovery ministry. The crucial issue is whether we're willing to practice deep confession.

Before probing further, we should acknowledge the awkward issue of ethnic exclusion. For good reason, we are uncomfortable to read that "those of Israelite descent separated themselves from all foreigners" (Neh. 9:2). Ethnic purity had been a major goal for Ezra, the supreme religious leader of Nehemiah's generation. He insisted that fellow Jews "separate yourselves from the peoples of the land and from the foreign wives" (Ezra 10:11). Such racial discrimination is anathema to us.

It's crucial to remember the historical context. Intermarriage risked the orthodox Jews' commitment to the true God, even if those foreigners were in the process of conversion. To Ezra and Nehemiah, this harsh and arbitrary practice seemed necessary to restore religious fidelity.[87] In contrast, during much of its history, Judaism welcomed the inclusion of Gentile converts.

Our context couldn't be more different than Nehemiah's. Christianity is a multiethnic faith. Intermarriage between ethnic groups can yield homes devoted to Christ as husbands and wives honor Jesus as Lord. Conversely, marriages within the same ethnic group can be divided on faith—more than a few believers are married to unbelievers. Such challenging family arrangements became common in the first century as the gospel took root in Jewish and Gentile households. How helpful to read Paul's gracious instruction to the early church:

> But I (not the Lord) say to the rest: If any brother has an unbelieving wife and she is willing to live with him, he must not divorce her. Also, if any woman has an unbelieving husband and he is willing to live with her, she must not divorce her husband. For the unbelieving husband is made holy by the wife, and the unbelieving wife is made holy by the husband. Otherwise your children would be unclean, but as it is they are holy.   1 Corinthians 7:12-14, CSB

Apostolic teaching wasn't only tolerant of mixed marriages. Pervading Paul's instructions was an enduring confidence that many unbelieving spouses would be positively influenced by the believing spouse. The gospel often prevailed within mixed marriages.

LOOKING BACK AND FACING FACTS

With this distinction in mind, let's glean insights from Nehemiah's account of public confession. In Nehemiah 9:3, we read that Jerusalem's Jews spent three hours listening to the Book of the Law and three hours "in confession and in worshipping." Afterwards, the Levites took turns leading the assembly in prayer, praising God for having "kept your promise" (9:8) . You can read this prayer for yourself in Nehemiah 9:5-31. In summary, it exalted the Lord who:

+ Created the vast heavens and this life-teeming planet
+ Chose to call Abram from idolatry to set apart a covenant people
+ Liberated their ancestors from Egyptian slavery
+ Blessed them with the revelation of God's Law
+ Sustained them through the wilderness
+ Brought them into the Promised Land
+ Forgave them for their disobedience
+ Sustained them in exile

For demonstrating enduring love despite their ancestors' unfaithfulness, the Water Gate assembly praised the Holy One with grateful hearts. Then with deep remorse, the Levites acknowledged the people's sinful legacy:

> "Now therefore, our God—the great and mighty and awesome God, keeping covenant and steadfast love—do not treat lightly all the hardship that has come upon us, upon our kings, our officials, our priests, our prophets, our ancestors, and all your people, since the time of the kings of Assyria until today. You have been just in all that has come upon us, for you have dealt faithfully and we have acted wickedly; our kings, our officials, our priests, and our ancestors have not kept your law or heeded the commandments and the warnings that you gave them. Even in their own kingdom, and in the great goodness you bestowed on them, and in the large and rich land that you set before them, they did not serve you and did not turn from their wicked works. Here we are, slaves to this day—slaves in the land that you gave to our ancestors to enjoy its fruit and its good gifts. Its rich yield goes to the kings whom you have set over us because of our sins; they have power also over our bodies and over our livestock at their pleasure, and we are in great distress."
>
> Because of all this we make a firm agreement in writing, and on that sealed document are inscribed the names of our officials, our Levites, and our priests.   Nehemiah 9:32-38

Jerusalem's Levites acknowledged the people's "great distress," for they continued to suffer the consequences of the evils committed by their ancestors, sin that they perpetuated (Neh. 9:37). Assurance of God's grace enabled them to pursue God's holiness. On behalf of God's people, they renewed their commitment to God's covenant: "making a binding agreement, putting it into writing...affixing our seals to it" (9:38).

Spiritual renewal and community restoration necessitate deep confession. Even though God has already adopted us as His forgiven children, our healing is facilitated by repentance. "Sackcloth and ashes" are not a prerequisite. What matters most is having absolute confidence in God's graciousness ("who keeps His covenant of love") while grieving sin's consequences ("we are in deep distress"). As stated previously, "the Gospel is bad news before it's good news."[88] To fully experience God's grace, we must face our guilt. God's unconditional acceptance cultivates deep confession and profound transformation.

RECOGNIZE IDOLS

Deep confession involves discerning and declaring our specific sins. Such repentance requires us to name the idols we are prone to worship, whether pleasure, success, money, beauty, family, ideology, leisure, or personal fulfillment. Deep confession requires us to acknowledge our tendency to be driven by appetites, compulsions, or addictions. Deep confession recognizes our inability to express unconditional love towards family, friends, and neighbors. Deep confession also recognizes that the legacy of past sin contributes to present injustice. As the Jews of Nehemiah's day confessed the sins of their ancestors, we should unflinchingly acknowledge our ancestors' sins. Family trees often yield sour fruit.

At issue isn't whether a few relatives might have been scoundrels. More important is to confess the scandal that our socially respectable ancestors may have participated in the mistreatment of minorities, the denigration of women, the cover-up of sexual abuse, exploitation of the poor, perhaps even the defense of slavery and the genocide of Native Americans. As God's covenant people, we should acknowledge their sin, lest we perpetuate their self-deception. If we name their sin, we are less likely to replicate it.

Among my prized possessions are a Presbyterian hymnal printed in 1867 in Richmond, Virginia, along with a silver Communion chalice. I inherited both from the DeVault side of my family—my French Huguenot ancestors. I'm also a descendant of Edward O. Guerrant, noted Confederate officer, physician, and post-Civil War evangelist in the Kentucky highlands. When I examine these artifacts, I appreciate my French Huguenot heritage. As Reformed Protestants in France, many Huguenots fled persecution as they emigrated to the American South. Yet I also wonder if they ever questioned their culture's racism.

Two of my ancestors provided contrasting glimpses of spiritual legacy. Aunt Grace lived up to her name, despite losing all three of her children to the 1918-1920 "Spanish Flu" Pandemic. Even as a child, I remember being profoundly impressed by her emotional strength and her gracious manner. Sadly, her sister—my Aunt Lulu—left the opposite impression. I distinctly remember her frequent use of racial slurs—even in the presence of an African American housekeeper. My parents didn't share such views or use such language. Nonetheless, in response my culture's racism, as a young man I asked the Lord to cleanse me from this toxic legacy. Deep confession continues, especially when seasons of national reckoning reveal my blind spots.

Deep confession yields personal liberation. Facing my racist heritage enables me to enjoy deep friendships with people of color.

Experiencing God's grace whets our desire to be more like Christ. As Peter wrote to the church, "set your hope completely on the grace to be brought to you at the revelation of Jesus Christ. As obedient children, do not be conformed to the desires of your former ignorance. But as the one who called you is holy, you also are to be holy in all your conduct" (1 Peter 1:13-15).

QUESTIONS TO PONDER:

1. Instead of "sackcloth and ashes," how should God's people practice "deep confession"?
2. How is trusting in God's unconditional grace a prerequisite for authentic confession?
3. Why was it important for the Levites to recall specifically their ancestors' past sins?
4. What aspects of your ancestral heritage hold you back from all that you could be?

DAY 39

COVENANTAL RESPONSIBILITY

Hope-building partnerships help people discover the benefit of covenant community.

Nehemiah not only restored and resettled a city. God used him to revive his neighbors' spirituality. Restoring the city increased their awareness of God's transformative presence. Hearing God's Word prompted their regret over sin. Assurance of God's grace cultivated their desire for holiness. Recognizing that past unfaithfulness brought about "great distress," Jerusalem's Jews renewed their commitment to God's covenant:

> "Because of all this we make a firm agreement in writing, and on that sealed document are inscribed the names of our officials, our Levites, and our priests."
>
> Nehemiah 9:38

The word "covenant" might recall HOA (Homeowner Association) rules that require people to keep landscapes neat and boat trailers hidden. This isn't the biblical definition. Neighborhood covenants are a shared set of obligations. Biblical covenants are premised on God's unconditional love, which enlarges our capacity to love God and people.

BIBLICAL COVENANTS

When providing premarital counseling, I enjoy shocking the engaged couple by explaining that in the eyes of the state, their marriage will be a contract enabling them to sue each other. That gets their attention! The Christian concept of marriage goes far beyond contractual expectations. Marriage isn't "a fifty-fifty proposition;" it's a commitment to forsake all others and devote yourselves to mutual betterment. This covenantal view of marriage reflects God's benevolent faithfulness.

The Lord makes and keeps covenants of grace. Divine initiatives permeate the scriptures. After resetting the created order with a flood, God told Noah that "I will establish my covenant with you," with the rainbow as its sign (Genesis 6:18; 9:12-13). After calling Abram out of Mesopotamia, the Lord renamed him "Abraham" as a foretaste of covenantal promises and expectations (Genesis 17:1-2).

Biblical covenants are purposeful. The promised blessing drew Abram into God's redemptive mission so that "through you all the people of the earth will be blessed" (Genesis 12:3). Rituals of remembrance (such as Sabbath, circumcision, and Passover) served to remind future generations of how the covenant-making God set them apart as a people, delivered them from bondage, sustained them in the wilderness, and led them into the Promised Land. When they strayed, the Lord raised up prophets to call them back to their covenantal obligations.

By returning them from exile in a second "exodus," God again liberated the Jews from oppression and brought them into a Promised Land. In parallel fashion, Nehemiah 10 describes a re-gifting of the Law in Jerusalem. (Initially given on Mt. Sinai.) Verses 1-27 lists the names of the leaders, Levites, and priests who seated this covenant (beginning with "Nehemiah the governor"). Starting with verse 28, we read about the setting and the specifics of covenantal renewal:

> The rest of the people, the priests, the Levites, the gatekeepers, the singers, the temple servants, and all who have separated themselves from the peoples of the lands to adhere to the law of God, their wives, their sons, their daughters, all who have knowledge and understanding, join with their kin, their nobles, and enter into a curse and an oath to walk in God's law, which was given by Moses the servant of God, and to observe and do all the commandments of the Lord our Lord and his ordinances and his statutes. We will not give our daughters to the peoples of the land or take their daughters for our sons; and if the peoples of the land bring in merchandise or any grain on the sabbath day to sell, we will not buy it from them on the sabbath or on a holy day; and we will forego the crops of the seventh year and the exaction of every debt.
>
> We also lay on ourselves the obligation to charge ourselves yearly one-third of a shekel for the service of the house of our God: for the rows of bread, the regular grain offering, the regular burnt offering, the sabbaths, the new moons, the appointed festivals, the sacred donations, and the sin offerings to make atonement for Israel, and for all the work of the house of our God...
>
> We obligate ourselves to bring the first fruits of our soil and the first fruits of all fruit of every tree, year by year, to the house of the Lord; also to bring to the house of our God, to the priests who minister in the house of our God, the firstborn of our sons and of our livestock, as it is written in the law, and the firstlings of our herds and of our flocks; and to bring the first of our dough, and our contributions, the fruit of every tree, the wine and the oil, to the priests, to

the chambers of the house of our God; and to bring to the Levites the tithes from our soil, for it is the Levites who collect the tithes in all our rural towns. And the priest, the descendant of Aaron, shall be with the Levites when the Levites receive the tithes; and the Levites shall bring up a tithe of the tithes to the house of our God, to the chambers of the storehouse. For the people of Israel and the sons of Levi shall bring the contribution of grain, wine, and oil to the store-rooms where the vessels of the sanctuary are, and where the priests that minister, and the gatekeepers and the singers are. We will not neglect the house of our God.　　　　Nehemiah 10:28-33, 35-39

Instead of simply restating the Law, this covenantal renewal focused on habits that transform good intentions into distinctive lifestyles. By ending intermarriage with idolatrous Gentiles, the Jews agreed not to risk future gen-erations' devotion to the one true God. By committing to a weekly Sabbath observance, they would enjoy God's rest and cultivate religious identity. By taking responsibility to provide offerings that sustained Temple operations, they would strengthen God-ordained religious institutions. Dedicating the first fruits that comprised a tithe (ten percent) of the harvest would demon-strate their trust that God would honor His promise to provide. In every aspect of ordinary life, each member of the covenant family pledged to honor God.

SACRAMENTAL COVENANT

Though Christians aren't bound by the Jewish religious law, covenantal principles gleaned from the Old Testament help to form our identity as God's adopted sons and daughters. Instead of circumcision, baptism functions as a sign and seal of this new covenant.[89] When baptism is administered, partici-pants remember God's promises and expectations. Baptism conveys the good news that "God loves you before you know it and will always love you—uncon-ditionally." This covenantal grace is embodied by the community. In congre-gations that encourage parents to present their children for baptism, members join parents in affirming a vow to share responsibility in nurturing the chil-dren's faith. In a church lobby, a teenager peeked at a recently baptized baby. He sheepishly explained, "If I'm responsible, I guess I should meet the kid."

Receiving the Sacrament of Holy Communion is another sign and seal of God's covenant, renewing our appreciation for Jesus' sacrificial love, which heals, strengthens, and sustains us for God's redemptive mission (Luke 22:20).

Sharing these sacred moments remind also renews our awareness of God's covenantal expectations. Though our culture fosters rampant individualism and discourages personal sacrifice, we dare to strengthen the ties that bind

Jesus-followers to each other. As we practice the fifty-nine New Testament "one-anothers" (i.e., "bear one another's burdens," Galatians 6:2), we honor Jesus and receive the mutual benefits of covenant community.

COVENANT COMMUNITY

Disappointment with church tempts people to withdraw from fellowship or select a congregation that function more like a "vendor of religious services and goods" than a spiritual family living God's mission.[90] Yet if we involve them in hope-building work, disillusioned people may glimpse of "church" as it was meant to be. As Jesus declared, "For where two or three are gathered together in my name, I am there among them" (Matthew 18:20, CSB).

To experience authentic Christian community involves covenantal obligations, including the commitment to wholehearted engagement, for we are "individual parts connected to each other" (Romans 12:5, ISV). We should "continue to consider how to motivate one another to love and good deeds, not neglecting to meet together" (Hebrews 10:24b-25a, ISV). As relationships deepen, disciples dare to discuss deeper aspects of how God covenantal expectations affect everyday life.

Written covenants can also cultivate profound missional aspirations. Conventional churches do well to invite newcomers to embrace a church membership covenant. For missionally-focused communities, written covenants communicate lifestyle expectations for disciples who partner in God's mission. The Underground Network is an entrepreneurial platform that cultivates micro- church expressions. Each micro-church has its own missional focus, yet each leader commits to a shared "Manifesto," aspiring to embody God's reign with lifestyle integrity.[91] Core participants in Church in the Wild are invited to embrace our Missional Disciple Aspirations (see Appendix).

Anticipate that your work will cultivate a renewed awareness of God's covenantal blessings and your fellow participants' willingness to experience covenant community. *The most enduring way to build hope is to let God use you to build the character of people with hope-building potential.*

QUESTIONS TO PONDER:

1. What were some of the obligations that Jerusalem's people embraced when they renewed their commitment to God's covenant?
2. What did you learn about the biblical concept of "covenant"?
3. How could your hope-building work help un-churched or de-churched people taste the rich blessing of Christian community?
4. Would your mission team or missional community benefit by composing a set of expectations/aspirations?

DAY 40

LEGACY ARRANGEMENTS

Our hope-building efforts can outlast us.

Nehemiah's last chapters testify to the positive momentum that continued as the governor prepared for others to lead after his departure. He had made the previous decision to resettle the city as a "tithe" of families from the surrounding region (Nehemiah 7:4). They had relocated into Jerusalem, "the holy city" (Neh. 11:1-2). Chapters 11 and 12 list dozens of men who brought their families, resulting in a cacophony of children's voices. Reading their names reminds us of Nehemiah's amazing impact on real people, as God channeled his holy discontent into blessing.

At the end of this census, Jerusalem's population celebrated God's goodness:

> Now at the dedication of the wall of Jerusalem they sought out the Levites in all their places, to bring them to Jerusalem to celebrate the dedication with rejoicing, with thanksgivings and with singing, with cymbals, harps, and lyres. The companies of the singers gathered together from the circuit around Jerusalem and from the villages of the Netophathites; also from Beth-gilgal and from the region of Geba and Azmaveth; for the singers had built for themselves villages around Jerusalem. Nehemiah 12:27-29

With great joy, the people praised God. While Nehemiah's role was obvious and people's sacrifices were evident, the citizens of Jerusalem recognized God's role in providing servant-hearted leaders and Spirit-united followers. They proceeded to dedicate the restored city to the Lord. Verse 30 tells us that "the priests and the Levites...purified themselves ceremonially" before "they purified the people, the gates, and the wall."

Verses 31-43 chronicle the worship service. Under the direction of Jezrahiah, two large choirs sang from atop the wall, accompanied by musical instruments (Neh. 12:42). Ezra led the procession, and "they offered great sacrifices, rejoicing because God had given them great joy. The women and the children also rejoiced. The sound of rejoicing in Jerusalem could be heard far away" (12:43).

What a memorable celebration! The remainder of Chapter 12 traces the assignment of duties that sustained leaders who provided for Jerusalem's spiritual and temporal welfare. Stewards were appointed to store "the contributions, first fruits and tithes," as well as to arrange the distribution of daily portions for priests, Levites, singers, and gatekeepers (12:44ff).

RESTORING THEOLOGICAL PURITY

The last chapter describes Nehemiah's attempt to tie down loose ends. When the Law of Moses was read at the consecration service, an oversight was discovered: the Law required that "no Ammonite or Moabite should ever be admitted into the assembly of God" (Neh. 13:1). Therefore, "they excluded from Israel all who were of foreign descent" (13:3). For the sake of preserving their religious heritage, the Jews returning from Mesopotamia set drastic boundaries on mingling with foreigners, even those converting to Judaism.

We should view Ezra's and Nehemiah's exclusion of foreigners as a short-term tactic that served God's long-term strategy of inclusion. Ethnic exclusion has not been typical of Judaism. During the previous period of the judges and early monarchy, the sagas of Ruth and Jonah encouraged Jews to view Gentiles as potential members of God's family. While in Babylonian exile, Isaiah prophesied the return of Jews to the Promised Land to initiate a trajectory of universal grace, to include everyone. According to Isaiah, God said:

> "It is too small a thing for you to be my servant,
> to raise up the tribes of Israel
> and bring back those of Jacob I have preserved.
> I'll also make you as a light to the nations,
> to be my salvation to the ends of the earth."   Isaiah 49:6, ISV

ONGOING VIGILANCE

Four hundred years later, Isaiah's vision was fulfilled when Jesus was recognized as "a light that will reveal salvation to unbelievers and bring glory to your people Israel" (Luke 2:32, ISV). In retrospect, it's apparent that Ezra's and Nehemiah's concern for religious purification was a temporary tactic. Striving for theological clarity by excluding Gentiles preceded the Jews' evangelistic mission to Gentiles.

The next verses tell how Nehemiah dealt with challenges to his authority. While reporting to King Artaxerxes in Persia, Eliashib the priest became "closely associated with Tobiah (Neh. 13:4). When Nehemiah returned,

> I then discovered the wrong that Eliashib had done on behalf
> of Tobiah, preparing a room for him in the courts of the house of
> God. And I was very angry, and I threw all the household furniture
> of Tobiah out of the room. Then I gave orders and they cleansed the

chambers, and I brought back the vessels of the house of God, with the grain offering and the frankincense.

I also found out that the portions of the Levites had not been given to them; so that the Levites and the singers, who had conducted the service, had gone back to their fields. So I remonstrated with the officials and said, "Why is the house of God forsaken?" And I gathered them together and set them in their stations. Then all Judah brought the tithe of the grain, wine, and oil into the storehouses. And I appointed as treasurers over the storehouses the priest Shelemiah, the scribe Zadok, and Pedaiah of the Levites, and as their assistant Hanan son of Zaccur son of Mattaniah, for they were considered faithful; and their duty was to distribute to their associates.   Nehemiah 13:7b-13

Effective leadership demands attentiveness and vigilance. "Tobiahs" will continue to conspire. Those people entrusted with authority will need correction. It's always necessary to cultivate the next generation of leaders. No matter the size of the organization, those who lead discover that "heavy is the head that wears the crown."[92] Leaders want to be liked, but it is far better that they be respected and take responsibility.

LEADERSHIP SERENITY

Many leaders feel conflicted about difficult decisions they must make in the process of hope-building. *More painful is our discovery that seeking to do good can yield conflict.* So how do we maintain our serenity? Focus on God's approval. Consider Nehemiah's prayer:

Remember me, O my God, concerning this, and do not wipe out my good deeds that I have done for the house of my God and for his service.   Nehemiah 13:14

Nehemiah's passion was to serve God as best he could. He didn't delude himself into thinking that he was infallible. Rather, he hoped that God would recognize his sincere, undivided heart. Implicit is Nehemiah's assumption of God's graciousness.

Even as the last section celebrated his leadership, Nehemiah couldn't relax and relish the fruits of his labor. Instead of tying up loose ends, he struggled to stop the unraveling of the social fabric. In verses 15-22, we read how Nehemiah confronted those people who violated the Sabbath by engaging in commerce when they should be worshiping God and resting. Only by locking them out of the city could he compel them to honor their Creator. The need to exert force affected Nehemiah's prayer for a righteous legacy. Instead of emphasizing his faithfulness, he shifted, appealing simply to God's grace:

> Remember this also in my favor, O my God, and spare me according to the greatness of your steadfast love.   Nehemiah 13:22b

Verses 23-28 tell us that the requirement for Jews to marry within their faith was also ignored: "I saw men of Judah who had married women from Ashdod, Ammon, and Moab."

> I contended with them and cursed them and beat some of them and pulled out their hair...And one of the sons of Jehoiada, son of the high priest Eliashib, was the son-in-law of Sanballat the Horonite; I chased him away from me.   Nehemiah 13:25, 28

Aware that his good intentions had devolved into abusive methods, he prayed for a righteous legacy. Nehemiah threw himself upon God's mercy:

> Remember me, my God, with favor.   Nehemiah 13:31b, ISV

Brothers and sisters, allowing God to channel your holy discontent into a passionate calling doesn't always yield contentment. Being a hope-builder not only involves personal sacrifice; it often leads to conflict. The seriousness that you bring to your sacred task may tempt you to be impatient with those who are lackadaisical. Zealous for positive change, you may be tempted to manipulate, even coerce.

Indeed, if you are passionate about a cause, those with whom you work might accuse you of emotional abusiveness. Such allegations could be sheer fabrications. Perhaps aspects of the accusations might have veracity, while being exaggerated by your enemies or repeated without context. Those accusing you might have misperceived your intentions and misjudged your heart. Sometimes the truth lies somewhere in the middle.

I have written candidly about my belief that cruelty and deceit led to my removal from pastoral leadership after twenty years of hope-building. Nonetheless, I recognize aspects of my own behavior in reading Nehemiah's zeal—not that anyone ever claimed that I "pulled out their hair" (Neh.13:25)! Yet in my zeal to build a vibrant, life-changing congregation, at times I was overly intense with fellow leaders, especially staff colleagues.

People in ministry leadership should have the humility to welcome critique and coaching. Many of my former colleagues shared these expectations and recognized that "iron sharpens iron" (Proverbs 27:17). When I was overbearing, most co-workers were strong enough to communicate their unhappiness in healthy ways. Sadly, a few of my former colleagues were unhealthy and acted in a passive aggressive manner. Unaware of their own vulnerability to Satan's designs, they manipulated ecclesiastical authorities to remove their brother and colleague, even as we were set to enter a conflict-resolution process. Nonetheless, I was not an "innocent victim."

As Christ-followers, we cannot rationalize intimidation tactics. We must aspire to lead like Jesus: he persuaded others to give themselves fully to God's work through prayer, vision casting, and his own example.

Nevertheless, if we are passionate in our hope-building, our brokenness will sometimes manifest itself as sin. If accused of abusiveness, our first impulse will be to justify ourselves, but if, like Nehemiah, our success is bathed in humility, *our ultimate satisfaction is not to celebrate our good works, but to relish God's grace.*

And whenever possible, we should strive to make peace (Hebrews 12:14).[93]

QUESTIONS TO PONDER:

1. What problems caused the community's progress to unravel?
2. What methods did Nehemiah use to ensure his legacy? Which ones are appropriate for Christ-followers? Which were abusive?
3. In what ways has your own hope-building been complicated by sins that you or others committed? Have you allowed yourself to relish God's grace?
4. Is there anyone to whom you should take the initiative in seeking reconciliation?

EPILOGUE

IMMEASURABLY MORE!

Halfway through his letter to the Ephesians, the Apostle Paul celebrated the magnificence of God's sovereign grace in this elegant prayer:

> I pray that he would give you, according to his glorious riches, strength in your inner being and power through his Spirit, and that the Messiah would make his home in your hearts through faith. Then, having been rooted and grounded in love, you will be able to understand, along with all the saints, what is wide, long, high, and deep— that is, you will know the love of the Messiah— which transcends knowledge, and will be filled with all the fullness of God.
>
> Now to the one who can do infinitely more than all we can ask or imagine according to the power that is working among us— to him be glory in the church and in the Messiah Jesus to all generations, forever and ever! Amen.   Ephesians 3:16-21, ISV

Your ability to accomplish God's purpose is dependent on "strength in your inner being and power through his Spirit" (Eph. 3:16, ISV). Our capacity to love grows from being "rooted and grounded in love" in the love of the Messiah" (3:19). As this power works within us, God accomplishes more than "all we ask or imagine," perhaps using us to intrigue non-believers (3:20).

Irene Summerford couldn't have imagined how the immense love of Christ would magnify the impact of her modest life. Growing up in the pre-civil rights racism of rural Florida and struggling with crushing poverty, no one would have expected that God would use her to forge diverse Christians, civic leaders, and a corporate CEO into a neighborhood development partnership.

When she moved to the Space Coast as a full-time mother of small children, Lynn Brockwell-Carey could have never imagined that God would position her to build a spiritually infused organization that transforms young lives and restores under-resourced communities. When she initially encountered the Booker T. Washington Neighborhood, Lynn didn't envision leading a team that would be called "the restorer of streets to live in" (Isaiah 58:12).

God can also do immeasurably more than all you ask or imagine. Failing to reach our goals does not mean that we misheard God or failed God. If we help others become disciples of Jesus, their potential for good is unlimited. As a proverb of unknown origin declares, "anyone can count the seeds in an apple, but no one can count the apples in a seed."

Amen!

WILD
FΛITH
PRESS

APPENDIX 1

MISSIONAL DISCIPLE ASPIRATIONS

As a sinner in need of God's grace, I continually place my trust in Jesus Christ as my Lord and Savior, expecting the Holy Spirit to make me more like Jesus as I turn from sin and strive to honor God in every aspect of my life.

As a steward of the Gospel, I will aspire to a lifestyle that manifests the grace of Jesus and advances God's mission:

- Setting aside time for spiritual reflection and Sabbath rest;
- Discerning the Spirit's guidance as I make consumer choices that impact whether I am available to give attention to God's work around me;
- Striving to have a public witness that honors Jesus' mission as my highest priority, I will use a gentle and constructive tone when making pronouncements regarding controversial issues, including social-media posts;
- Praying to be bold and Spirit-led in taking the initiative to befriend neighbors and be a blessing in my community and workplace;
- Practicing hospitality by taking the time to converse with neighbors, and when Spirit-led, to welcome them into my home;
- Seeking to use my time, talents, skills, and influence to advance the Kingdom of God; developing habits of generosity with my financial resources;
- Preparing for the opportunity to bless others by sharing my faith journey with those who show signs of openness to spiritual conversations.

As a disciple in need of Christian community, I will participate in fellowship and worship gatherings of *Church in the Wild*. Knowing that missional partnerships will inevitably yield conflicts:

- When I am disappointed with others, I will gently share my concerns directly with them, seeking to honor Christ with forbearance, mutual understanding, and reconciliation;
- If my concerns are not heeded, I will ask another Christian brother or sister to go with me as I attempt to speak the truth in love to the brother or sister who has offended me;
- If I discern that the Holy Spirit is leading me to end my participation in *Church in the Wild*; I will communicate this decision to one of its leaders.

ENDNOTES

[1] *Purpose-Driven Life* (Grand Rapids: Zondervan, 2002).

[2] Darrell Guder, *The Continuing Conversion of the Church* (Grand Rapids, Eerdmans Publishing Co., 2000), 131.

[3] "In U.S., Decline of Christianity Happens at a Rapid Pace," Pew Research Center, October 17, 2019, www.pewforum.org/2019/10/17/in-u-s-decline-of-christianity-continues-at-rapid-pace/.

[4] "Are All These Christians' Complaints of Religious Discrimination Just So Much Empty Whining?" http://www.beliefnet.com/faiths/home-page-news-and-views/are-all-these-christians-complaints-of-religious-discrimination-just-so-much-empty-whining.aspx?.

[5] Dallas Willard, *The Divine Conspiracy: Rediscovering Our Hidden Life in God* (New York: HarperCollins, 1998), 41.

[6] The first settlers to return to Jerusalem were led by Sheshbazzar. Twenty-one years later the Persian king sent Ezra, a Jewish priest. Ezra's mission was to restore true worship practices and challenge Jewish families to be faithful to the one true God. A few years later Zerrubbabel led effort to construct a new Temple, which was finished in 520 BC. During this period the Lord directed His people through the prophetic teaching of Haggai and Zechariah. Several generations later Nehemiah received his call (445 B.C.).

[7] Jim Collins, *Good to Great* (New York: Harper Business, 2001), 51.

[8] *Glory to God: The Presbyterian Hymnal* (Louisville: Westminster John Knox Press, 2013), No. 625.

[9] *Reflections on the Psalms* (New York: Harcourt, Brace & Co., 1958), pp. 93–97.

[10] "Tractates on the Gospel of John, *Tractate XII on John 3:6-21*, www.azquotes.com/author/663-Saint_Augustine/tag/confession..

[11] *Take Words With You: A Manual for Intercession* (Compiled by Tim Kerr, 2010), 5, www.challies.com/christian-living/take-words-with-you/.

[12] Erwin McManus, *An Unstoppable Force: Daring to Be the Church that God Had in Mind* (Loveland, CO: Group, 2001), 32-33.

[13] Brevard Neighborhood Development Association was renamed Neighbor Up Brevard in 2018.

[14] Author's recollection of address Rick Warren gave in 1998 at the Purpose Driven Church Conference, Saddleback Community Church, Lake Forest, CA.

[15] Recounted on Days 22 and 26.

[16]Harold K. Moulton, ed., *The Analytical Greek Lexicon Revised* (Grand Rapids: Zondervan Publishing House, 1978), 47.

[17]Guder, 106-119

[18]See Lance Ford and Brad Brisco, *Next Door as it is in Heaven: Living Out God's Kingdom in your Neighborhood* (Colorado Springs: NavPress, 2016).

[19]Helpful resources for spiritual discernment include Michael Frost, *Surprise the World: The Five Habits of Highly Missional People* (Colorado Springs, CO: NavPress, 2016); Hugh Halter and Matt Smay, *The Tangible Kingdom Primer* (Uniontown, OH: Missio Publishing, 2009).

[20]Wayne Gordon and John M. Perkins, *Making Neighborhoods Whole: A Handbook for Christian Community Development* (Downer's Grove, IL: InterVarsity Press, 2013), 33.

[21]*Wishful Thinking: A Seeker's ABC* (New York: HarperOne, 1993), 118.

[22]More insights arising from our journey to cultivate Church in the Wild will be shared on Days 17, 25, 27, and 39. The concept of a missional (outwardly-focused) church was introduced on Day 6.

[23]To train participants and allow them ample time to participate in missional micro-church communities, Church in the Wild limits worship gatherings to two Sundays a month and provides WildLife—a micro-church training experience—on alternate Sundays.

[24]quoteinvestigator.com/2020/05/13/make-friends/

[25]Richard M. Nixon, *Six Crises* (New York: A Cardinal Edition: Pocket Books, 1962), p. 253.

[26]Stephen R. Covey, *Seven Habits of Highly Effective People* (New York: Simon & Schuster, 1989), 255.

[27]Jim Collins, *Good to Great: Why Some Companies Make the Leap…and Others Don't* (New York: HarperCollins, 2001), 70.

[28]http://malphursgroup.com/state-of-the-american-church-plateaued-declining/.

[29]The overview of Jerusalem's gates is reprinted from https://sentarmeenunanube.blogspot.com/2017/05/walls-of-jerusalem-nehemiah-map.html The model of Jerusalem is from www.ritmeyer.com.

[30]Robert D. Lupton, *Toxic Charity: How Churches and Charities Hurt Those They Seek to Help* (New York: HarperCollins, 2011).

[31]Millard Fuller, *More Than Houses: How Habitat for Humanity is Transforming Lives and Neighborhoods* (Nashville: Word Publishing, 2000), 40.

[32]Taylor Branch, *Parting the Waters: America in the King Years, 1954-63* (New York: Simon & Schuster, 1988); 4, 454-465.

[33]While its origins are uncertain, the proverb likely comes from Africa: https://www.npr.org/sections/goatsandsoda/2016/07/30/487925796/it-takes-a-village-to-determine-the-origins-of-an-african-proverb

[34]Rick Warren, *Purpose Driven Life* (Grand Rapids, Zondervan, 2002), 83.

[35]Mike and Sally Breen, *Family on Mission: Integrating Discipleship into the Fabric of our Everyday Lives* (Pawley's Island, South Carolina: 3DM Publishing, 2014), 10.

[36]For more information on missional communities, see Reggie McNeal, *Missional Communities: The Rise of the Post-Congregational Church* (San Francisco: Jossey-Bass, 2011) and Mike Breen, *Leading Missional Communities: Rediscovering the Power of Living on Mission Together* (Pawley's Island, South Carolina: 3DM Publishing, 2013).

[37]Lance Ford, Rob Wegner, Alan Hirsch, *The Starfish and the Spirit: Unleashing the Leadership Potential of Church and Organizations* (Grand Rapids: Zondervan Reflective, 2021), 101.

[38]Ford, Wegner, and Hirsch, *The Starfish and the Spirit,* 101.

[39]Eric Metcalf, et. al., *Developing an Apprentice* (Chicago: Community Christian Church, 2014).

[40]The testimony of a workshop leader at a training conference at Christ's Community Church of Chicago in the early 2000s (person unknown and date uncertain).

[41]https://www.physicsclassroom.com/class/newtlaws/Lesson-4/Newton-s-Third-Law

[42]John Craig, "Wesleyan Baccalaureate Is Delivered by Dr. King," *Hartford Courant,* June 8, 1964, 4.

[43]Arbinger Institute, *Leadership and Self-Deception: Getting Out of the Box,* 2nd Ed. (San Francisco: Berrett Koehler Publishers, 2010), xii.

[44]The name of Dan B. Allender's remarkable account of personal growth, informed by the story of Jacob, whose name meant "he who trips you up." God renamed him Israel ("one who struggles with God") after he suffered the consequences of his manipulation. *Leading with a Limp* (Colorado Springs: WaterBrook Press, 2015).

[45]Franklin D. Roosevelt, Inaugural Address, March 4, 1933.

[46]McManus, 33.

[47]William Safire, "Keeping Your Powder Dry" in *New York Times Magazine* (February 23, 1997), 20.

[48]Philip Yancey, *Finding God in Unexpected Places* (New York: Penguin Random House, 2008), 242.

[49]Linda J. Dahlberg, Robin M. Ikeda, and Marcie-jo Kresnow, "Guns in the Home and Risk of a Violent Death in the Home: Findings from a National Study" in *American Journal of Epidemiology* (Volume 160, Issue 10, November 15, 2004), 929-936.

[50]John Gramlich, "Five Facts About Crime in the U.S." Pew Research Center (January 30, 2018) http://www.pewresearch.org/fact-tank/2018/01/30/5-facts-about-crime-in-the-u-s/.

[51]As Michael Breen observed from Luke 6:12-19, "Jesus lived out his life in three relationships: Up—with his Father; In—with his chosen followers; Out—with the hurting world around him. This three-dimensional pattern for living a balanced life is evident throughout Scripture." *Building a Discipleship Culture* (Pawley's Island, South Carolina: 3DM Publishing, 2014), 3rd ed., 92.

[52]"Unchurched" refers to those who lack meaningful participation in Christian community—whether they still hold to the Christian faith or are skeptics. "De-churched" refers to those who were meaningfully engaged in a church but have dropped out due to disappointment or difficult circumstances.

[53]https://www.jimcollins.com/concepts/level-five-leadership.html

[54]See Day 22.

[55]John V. Winings, *Mountain Majesty: The History of CODEP Haiti—Where Sustainable Agricultural Development Works* (Sonoita, AZ: Dudley Court Press, 2016).

[56]https://theworld.org/stories/2014-03-07/suzanne-massie-taught-president-ronald-reagan-important-russian-phrase-trust.

[57]Isaiah 14:12-14.

[58]C.S. Lewis, *The Screwtape Letters* (London: Geoffrey Bles, 1942), 3.

[59]Wikipedia article on "Computer Virus," with reference to William Stallings, *Computer Security: Principles and Practice* (Boston: Pearson, 2012), 182.

[60]Insights regarding the literal and figurative aspects of the armor worn by Roman soldiers has been informed by Markus Barth, *Ephesians 4-6, The Anchor Bible* (Garden City, NY: Doubleday and Co., 1960), 766-777.

[61]John Wesley, *Explanatory Notes on the New Testament* (London: Epworth Press, 1958), 722.

[62]From the Bill and Melinda Gates Foundation Vision Statement.

[63]https://economics.mit.edu/files/1785

[64]https://www.supremecourt.gov/about/figuresofjustice.pdf

[65]Annie Kelly, "Latest Figures Reveal that More than 40 Million People Living in Slavery," *The Guardian*, September 19, 2017.

[66]Sidney Homer and Richard Sylla, *A History of Interest Rates*, 4th Ed. (Hoboken, New Jersey: John Wiley & Sons, 2005), 31.

[67]"The Negro is Your Brother," *The Atlantic Monthly*, Aug. 1963; Vol. 212, No. 2, 78 - 88.

[68]The Jewish observation of the Year of Jubilee is described in Leviticus 25:8-13.

[69]Millard Fuller and Diane Scott, *Love in the Mortar Joints: The Story of Habitat for Humanity* (Clinton, N.J.: New Win Publishing, Inc., 1980).

[70]Robert Penn Warren, *All the Kings Men* (New York: Harcourt Brace, 1946).

[71]http://beliefnet.com/faiths/christianity/2005/10/rick-warrens-second-reformation.aspx2.

[72]Day 16

[73]https://lifeclub.org/books/diffusion-of-innovations-everett-m-rogers-review-summary.

[74]Robert Lupton, *Renewing the City: Reflections on Community Development and Urban Renewal* (Downers Grove: InterVarsity Press, 2005), 172-173.

[75]The same names are listed in Ezra 2:3-61.

[76]Guder, 131.

[77]Steve Corbett and Brian Fikkert, *When Helping Hurts: How to Alleviate Poverty Without Hurting the Poor and Yourself* (Chicago: Moody Publishers, 2009).

[78]Stanley Hauerwas and William Willimon, *Resident Aliens, Life in Christian Community: A Provocative Christian Assessment of Culture and Ministry for People who Know that Something is Wrong*, 25th Anniversary Ed (Nashville, Abingdon Publishing, 2014), Preface.

[79]Leslie Newbigin, *The Gospel in a Pluralistic Society* (Grand Rapids, Eerdmans Publishing Co., 1989), 8-13.

[80]William Watkinson, "The Invisible Strategy" in *The Supreme Conquest, and Other Sermons* (New York: Fleming H. Revell Co., 1907), 218.

[81]The NIV Study Bible. Kenneth Barker, general editor (Grand Rapids: Zondervan, 1995), 667.

[82]Jacob Myers, *The Anchor Bible: Ezra and Nehemiah* (Garden City, NY: Doubleday & Company, 1965), 154.

[83]https://www.dbsguide.org.

[84]Greg Ogden, *Transforming Discipleship: Making Disciples a Few at a Time* (Downer's Grove, IL: InterVarsity Press, 2003). Other resources to consider include: Tim Keller,

Gospel in Life (Grand Rapids, Zondervan, 2010); Jeff Vanderstelt, *Saturate: Being Disciples of Jesus in the Everyday Stuff of Life* (Wheaton, IL: Crossway, 2015); Robert Thune and Will Walker, *The Gospel-Centered Life* (Greensboro, NC: New Growth Press, 2011).

[85]https://www.aa.org/assets/en_US/smf-121_en.pdf.

[86]Frederick Buechner, *Telling the Truth: The Gospel as Tragedy, Comedy, and Fairy Tale* (San Francisco: Harper & Row, 1977), 7.

[87]Arthur J. Wolak explains that "in an era when established religious conversions were not yet practiced, boundary maintenance could be more effectively achieved along ethnic lines. Thus, acceptance of the notion of ethnic boundaries seems to have been essential for Ezra's edict to take hold," from "Ezra's Radical Solution to Judean Assimilation" in *Jewish Bible Quarterly* Vol. 40 (November 2, 2012): 102.

[88]Buechner, 7.

[89]"The days are surely coming, says the Lord, when I will make a new covenant with the house of Israel and the house of Judah" (Jeremiah 31:31). Jeremiah's prediction was fulfilled in Jesus, for "How much more will the blood of Christ, who through the eternal Spirit offered himself without blemish to God, cleanse our consciences from dead works so that we can serve the living God? Therefore, he is the mediator of a new covenant…" (Hebrews 9:14-15a, CSB).

[90]George R. Hunsberger, "Sizing Up the Shape of the Church," in *The Church Between Gospel and Culture: The Emerging Mission in North America,"* ed. George R. Hunsberger and Craig Van Gelder (Grand Rapids, Eerdmans Publishing Co., 1996):333-346.

[91]Brian Sanders, *Underground Church* (Grand Rapid: Zondervan, 2018): 251-262.

[92]Derived from "uneasy is the head that wears a crown," William Shakespeare, *Henry IV, Part 2* (Act 3, Scene1, Line 31); found in https://shakespeare.folger.edu/shakespeares-works/henry-iv-part-2/act-3-scene-1/.

[93]This book has become an invaluable treasure for learning to prevent and defuse conflict: Ken Sande, *The Peacemaker: A Biblical Guide to Resolving Personal Conflict* (Grand Rapids: Baker Books, 2004).

ABOUT THE AUTHOR

Michael Carey leads Church in the Wild, a family of missional disciples on Florida's "Space Coast." While serving as a senior pastor of a conventional congregation, he founded the Presbyterians Seeking Purpose-Driven Ministry Conference and received Saddleback Community Church's Purpose-Driven Champion award. Michael is married to Lynn Brockwell-Carey, the founding Director of Neighbor Up Brevard, a Christian community development organization that operates The DOCK, an after-school program, where Michael teaches JAM (Jesus and Me) and leads the Garden Club.

Made in USA - Kendallville, IN
51181_9780578869124
07.21.2022 1629